Tokyo Poetry Journal

Vol. 14

Eros

Subscriptions available via our website (credit card, Paypal, bank transfer, or international postal money order sent to address below). ¥1500/issue or ¥2500/year for individuals, ¥2500/issue or ¥3500/year for institutions. Make bank transfers to: Japan Post Bank
 (Account Name: Johnson Jeffrey Richard, Bank Code 10020, Branch# 008, Account# 24951451).

www.topojo.com
facebook.com/tokyopoetryjournal
soundcloud.com/youtube-topojo
Instagram: @tokyopoetry
Twitter: @PoetryTokyo
ISBN 978-1-957704-09-8

CONTENTS

Introduction

There can be a sense of risk when it comes to sharing personal expressions of love or sex in something as concrete as the written form.

The sheer permanence of it can rattle.

Getting naked is one thing—but what if you have to be naked forever?

Jeffrey Johnson, Editor-in-Chief of the Tokyo Poetry Journal, told me that he used to write love poems on napkins and slip them hopefully to women in bars, essentially disclaiming ownership of the verse the moment it left his hand. Myself, I would write my teenage love poems in pencil only, safe in the knowledge that my feelings could be erased in an emergency.

In a more global sense, erotic writing has been subject to countless restrictions since the dawn of literature. Ovid's *The Art of Love* was banned for over 2,000 years. Theosophist renegade Annie Besant was jailed in 1877 for the distribution of obscene material deemed too racy for public consumption (the topic: contraception advice for working-class women). The most famous examples in this vein are arguably Oscar Wilde and Allen Ginsberg, yet there are countless lesser known but equally fascinating cases—take Lenore Kandel, psychedelic sex poet of the Beat Generation, whose 1966 *To Fuck With Love*, which she defined as "holy erotica", was instead deemed obscene by the courts. (Cementing Kandel's badass status: the sudden surge in sales after this verdict prompted her to donate 1% of the profits to the Police Retirement Association, in gratitude.) More recently in Japan, the manga artist Megumi Igarashi was arrested in 2014 for "distributing obscene data" in the form of a 3D scan of her vulva, which she constructed into an actual kayak and took on a maiden voyage down the Tama River in Tokyo. Her subsequent legal battles elegantly underscore the fear still evoked by depictions of the vagina, at least when it is a woman herself who is doing the depicting.

What is it about sex that threatens lawmakers so? The visionary comic book writer and ceremonial magician Alan Moore has argued that an activity as basic as masturbation terrifies political and religious institutions for the simple fact that it cannot be monetized, and thus represents a deadly threat to the very fabric of our culture and the ways in which it can be controlled. And governmental forces aren't the only ones who try to control self-expression: well-meaning family groups do it, a polite and well-functioning society does it, and more often than not, after absorbing these influences and swirling them together with our own doubts about the safety of being vulnerable, we do it to ourselves.

Despite such fears, poets have historically been unable to resist the call of Eros. Anais Nin, celebrated diarist and unparalleled sexual iconoclast who was known to frequent Parisian whorehouses with consort Henry Miller in the 1930s, and who occasionally wrote pulp erotica for dirty magazines to pay the bills, maintained that we write to taste life twice: in the moment and in retrospection.

So perhaps poets are merely hungry. Perhaps tasting the carnal just once is not enough. And perhaps the flavor of lust on the tongue only increases in potency when it is shared—societal restraints be damned.

The works in this volume are full of tastes—and tongues, and lusts, and all the accoutrements that go with them. We are treated to the sensuality of figs, pomegranates, honey, and other delicacies of the body. We are invited to brush our fingertips across countless shoulder blades and thighs and throats, and to tremble before them in fear or in worship. And much like the god Eros himself, who was alternately praised as a playful romantic and reviled as a cruel trickster, we are cautioned to be open-minded in our interpretations of what constitutes the erotic. You will read nearly as many works on loneliness here as on ecstasy, and tender love poems coexist side-by-side with tawdry ones.

Much of this volume may titillate. However, at its heart, the works herein represent a kaleidoscope of the human sexual experience in the early 21st century—stripped of shame, stripped of taboo, and stripped of any of the uncertainties that might prevent one from celebrating their vision of Eros.

So yes, it's a strip show in a sense—sometimes an erotic one; sometimes more bizarre—and in another, it's a symbol of the purity we can attain when we allow our very souls to be naked.

Joy Waller
December 2023

Eros

SAYAKA ASABA
translated by Jordan A. Y. Smith

In the Town of Machida

You must not go to the other side of the railroad tracks
They warn all the kids in Machida, I'm told

Because nasty adults   are doing nasty things

A band member   now
Wanna make some noise
I say,   so he scatters some praise my way
I say,   so it's karaoke time
Like all you can eat soft-serve ice cream
Sweet maudlin singing voice   it's love, but
A three-hour session won't be enough
I've gotten old   he says, drooping
That's right,
You're an old man, aren't you?

My dreams go unabated,
though they do have an expiry date
I've memorized   one stanza of a song with fingerprint-smeared lyrics
Those dudes   probably memorized it too:
the lifestyles of people who amount to less than a handful

At the tracks by the south entrance,
Let's play dirty
Command my breathing
with your beloved Zippo
Same cigarette brand
as my dad

How to play the guitar
How to throw darts
Also, oolong tea with Baileys
It's alright   at this point––
Also how to make out, how to make love—
teach me everything

You treat me like a child, but those
Throwaway social media shouts, selfies with your guitar—
You're an idiot too.
Do some work, you NEET
You're so adorable I don't even care
Someday   if you
grow to fit into
some sleepy residential area

I'll be playing nasty
across those railroad tracks by the south entrance

JOHN SOLT

Untitled

there's something raw
pulsating between us

after the aphrodisiac
sandy asses on the beach

what you do to me
and for me
intersect

even while you sleep
you're my dream

Untitled

after the bath
i dried you off
with my tongue

PD LYONS

Sister Stones

Today I brought her stones
sister stones
white round found together on the beach

Not the waxy white
not glassy grey
but almost opal

Round

Alike

Together

Put into her wet
from my having sucked their salt

White

T-shirt like a too short dress
occasional exposures of hair
as I walk across the room

stop
You kneel
inhale
Breathe long against me
Put your mouth to me

I lean
Again
I lean
Again
Squeeze
Draw me in
Again
This time wide opening with your tongue

Fallow

Not vaginal anal nipple sucking wild
Rather shoulders touching
Hand holding
As long as soft sheltered land spills into water
Breath deep effortless as the horizon
Glowing

ILIAS TSAGAS

The Polygender

The year is 2723 and I am a cisgender man. Historians say the term was first used around 700 hundred years ago.

But the talk of our Alps is the polygenders. Sexual encounters with them promise to be an intergalactic experience.

Polygenders are known for their black holes, formed in either their right or left arms. These are the farthest humans can reach out in the universe. The other genders will penetrate the hole and quickly get sucked into it, transported to the outer Alps.

The immense beauty of space reveals itself: glittering stars, orgasmic constellations expelling dust and gas of aging stars, and trembling in the birth of new ones.

Nobody knew about it. Because the first men and women who penetrated the black holes never returned. Polygenders kept it a secret out of fear and others didn't consider it important for polygenders attracted misfits and deviants, who nobody sought or missed.

Until I decided to try.

I was quickly transported to space, covered by the dust of lost information, things my ancestors did, sentiments and emotions I had forgotten I had. I floated and floated, enjoying the light. And after years of travelling and information catching I came across a lost, historic tune and rode its sound waves, singing:

Yes, only love can break your heart
Yes, only love can break your heart. *

A massive earthquake shook Earth. The polygenders started shaking, letting out sounds of fear and orgasmic relief. I was expelled from the nebulas back on to Earth.

I spread the news and now humans seek love into the most unexpected places.

(*) The text in italics are lyrics written by Neil Young for his song "Only Love Can Break Your Heart". The song is listed in Young's *After the Gold Rush* studio album, released in 1970.

I'm Connected: A Grid Orgasm

.com to order Domino's pizza, .com to have it delivered, so I spare time for .com chatting, I get tired of the online nude, I allow the network to enter me, my body has router spasms, .com penetrates me and I penetrate it back, my sex flows through the electromagnetic roots, there is no Wi-Fi pathway that does not feed my desires, no desires that do not infiltrate the matrix; I have fucked the network.

Paris Night Out

When looking for sex among the Algerians, the Moroccans, and other migrants of dubious status, he likes to take note of their underwear brands. Kelvin Klein is one, Calvin Klain is another common one. A reminder of his reliance on substitutes.

DAVORD GRIFFITHS

Mortal, again
(—a rejoinder to James K. Baxter's "Haast Pass")[1]

Crushed bark exudes mortality; lost—
Dislocated, the fern frond mocks my new arrival: It curls, drops spores, and
Clutches.
Yakushima crone splits root and leaf of cedar
Upon stony hearth: ancient song rises from chapped
Lips: "Kalyi lag, kalyi lag. Priap, slarnhak."

Still the frond turns away indifferent. Stoat cries out its newfound
Brotherhood. Fire crackles, spits; rock glows
Incandescent, and who am I? Prometheus, forever denied Olympus—
Alone, I accept my little deaths, too, like

Stones.

---

[1]   James K. Baxter Selected Poems. JE Weir ed. (Oxford University Press. 1985), p. 7.

DAISUKE YAKUMO

Fine

I hear you've drifted to a new town
You're starting over there for the first of many times
Is it a nice place?
Are the people friendly?

I hope you don't feel like it's someone else's fault
that things don't work out anymore
Sometimes you might have to deal with crap again

It's nobody's fault
That's the way crap is

The sunset was so beautiful that I was fine with the way it ended
Everywhere becomes a special place

I put the tobacco leaves on the paper, set the filter, rolled it up in one go, and lit it
Then I inhaled and exhaled the smoke along with the rumors

Azuma-bashi bridge
The Sumida River and the sun meld together

Rimbaud died long ago

And I can't find any more words to say

It's a good day to forget you

Pilgrimage

Went to Père-Lachaise
And to City Lights Books
Climbed the Acropolis
Went to Tijuana, got drunk on tequila, sex, and marijuana
Was dazzled by the Mayan pyramids of the Yucatan
Prayed in Bethlehem
Wandered in Palestine
Mesmerized by the Scandinavian midnight sun

I have passed through ancient deserts
I have come to the Cape of Good Hope

But it's different
It's different

    "No one will love me"
    "They'll all disappear, leaving me behind"

I hold you silently and tightly
letting the helpless words abort on my tongue

I know one day I will lose you again
I know I will return to the streets as a wanderer
I will go to the city you loved with the flowers I couldn't give
I will go to the sea you loved with the tears I couldn't shed

Unhappy little girl blue
Nina Simone is playing the refrain over and over in my head

You are a pale, fleeting presence that will soon be forgotten
But at the same time, you are eternal

And I'm on my way to Graceland

The path I have taken
Becomes a constellation named you

You are my pilgrimage

JES KALLED

Untitled

I met the ocean, I said
he asked how it felt to dance at dawn
in the ice cold waves of May
I asked him, *what did I look like?*
His camera searched for me, he said
I had sand in my ears then

We found a coin shower next to a seven eleven in the middle of nowhere
I used three coins for the hot water, had to ask it to come
to wash away the cold
the meeting
and the cold
The shaking
In the car we sat silently, driving past green rice fields
wet and lush
I was dry and warm by then, holding a bottle of hot tea
I haven't felt such wild calm
in a while

Sun difference

Beads of sweat pass over my collarbone
travel
down the center of my chest
wet and
round

It is not yet summer
But I know those long days of sound,
the deep breathing of birds and bugs as they live, live, live
so loudly
in wet heat
I was a child when we met and I knew nothing of people
Didn't understand why they got angry
or what they wanted

The dirt from the garden was on my knees and on my cheek
When I lay in the grass, ants walked all over and bit me sometimes, I didn't like that
The sun, yellow, yellow like a lemon
I licked my arm because I wanted to taste the difference—what the sun did to it

Notes to Samson

When I open something with my hands,
alone, sometimes I realize I am also
with everyone else I've loved—they are
with me. Maybe Memory slips inside
openings, and stays. None of you go.
It's actually rather hard to have you all
here, wondering if your importance
is imagined, and magnified, or if it's
something more complex and magical
than what we usually allow ourselves to
consider.

I still think about you on days when the
moon is full, and no one else is. This isn't
a confession, it's a Notation.

Thomas, I never told you of the
dissonance, because I didn't know how
much there was, and when I realized, I
didn't think you could hold it. I notice
how sometimes you ask me to hold your
backpack, or your drink. It always feels
awkward, and on purpose. Can you hold
this? You ask. Knowing that I will.

A, I'm quite sure you disrupted my sense
of belonging, and that you have no idea
nor intention of caring. One of the last
times we spoke at length, you asked me
to go for a walk. You had just moved
into my apartment building, the room
below mine. You smiled when you said
your girlfriend didn't like that. You said
your dream was to be holding a glass
of wine, while your kids ran around, in
your wake, playing. Your wife would take
care of them and you would nurse the
glass. You didn't love your girlfriend, you
said, and you didn't know why. Maybe

you would marry her though, you said,
because she listened.

F, I woke up from a nightmare the other
night, whimpering. Dream You said,
It's easier for me, when I see that you're
doing terribly. Last night, Dream You
said very little. You cut out photos of us
and pasted them onto your schedule,
which was public. Like a carousel.

Samson, sometimes I imagine writing
to you, and asking to meet, but I
haven't done so. It's a hesitation that's
oscillated for 10 years. I had forgotten
closeness, until I went back and read
our old correspondence. I want to ask
you why you left, and if you ever found
your answers. You look happy in your
recent photos, and still have that edge
of independence. In your last email, you
write about Reality and Expectation, and
how we spoke of this when we first met.
I thought we were by the railroad tracks,
not on a bench like you say.
    EXT. - NIGHT - I said I didn't
like the endings of movies because they
seemed like lies, and lies are things that
starve us. A girl we both knew (with eyes
so bright and blue that her name in my
phone was not a name but the only blue
flower found on a vodafone) whispered,
Please don't ever change. I wanted to
ask her, what do you mean? And put
her words somewhere safe until I could
figure them out. Beau had said the same
thing when I left.

Beau, I have this one memory in my
truck, where I'm driving, and you're in
the passenger seat. We were so free back

then, though we didn't feel it. You rolled down the window and shouted, WE HAVE THE BEST SEX, to try to break the frame that kept us inside. I don't have my grandmother's truck anymore. Nor my grandmother. Nor you. When you wrote to me after years of nothing, it meant everything. It made people seem more like movement and less like salt. Maybe love has nothing to do with other people, just salt, and where God puts the salt. Into Lakes and Sweating Bodies.

I once broke the window in your bedroom by accident, you quickly pulled my hand away from the glass and searched my palms to see if He was there. Ad infinitum. People repeat the words they often hear. We give them to other people and don't know what they mean. Words like, I love you, don't change, and Amen. The only way to tell if someone loves you is to be yourself.

RACHEL FERGUSON

Shared Sleep

"Love does not make itself known through the desire for copulation...but in the desire
for shared sleep."
—Milan Kundera, *The Unbearable Lightness of Being*

You say you cannot sleep when we're too close
or face to face;
always turn away, not through choice
but necessity;
just can't settle down when your skin
is touching skin.
It's you.
Not me.
I must not take it personally.

After making love, you kiss me once,
squeeze me—
a firm full stop.
Then,
almost immediately,
              roll, roll, away
                       (an arm's length away but it feels so

         far away)
and drift off
easily.

Unknown to you, love,
then comes the disloyalty:
your body betrays you
with brazen discourtesy.

A leg snakes back.
Toes outstretched,
your foot finds my foot
and they dance
a slow serpentine dance
before our ankles hook.

Sunflower to the sun you turn,
take hold of my thigh.
I hold
my breath...
            and watch until...
                    your brow smooths...
                            you sigh ....

and I get what I've been waiting for:
your thinking self erased,
in one clean sweep you bind me,
wrap your arm around my waist,
your hands cradles curves,
my hip welds to your chest and
when each limb is interlaced,
your head lays on my breast.

Here you sleep.
Here you dream.
Here you are confessed.

Oysters

the invitation
slippery, salty, savory
glides along my tongue

Anatomy of a Kiss

The nexus of reactions begins
with a spike in thermal energy:
temperatures rise, pulses trip,
stomachs have been known to flip
as two distinct psyches agree,
locking eyes, wordlessly,
that what might happen
will indeed occur.

Moving closer, scents are sensed.
First, top notes of perfumes, laundry soap.
Under those, the true essence:
deep base notes
of pheromones.

Vibrations might be observed now,
charged particles thickening
the slice of space
between two souls,
taunting them to touch.

So touch

my shoulder,
slope of my spine,
lay hold of my head,
fingers laced in tangled strands,
pull me close,
taste my breath,

lick your lips,
avow the secret of your mouth,

oh god,
kiss me softly,
softer than the scent of apples
in an orchard at sunset
in September,

slowly,

slower,

now slip your tongue,
that blind self-governed beast
just past my teeth,
let it search for meaning
in a place where none exists
and never quit—

this could be love

or dopamine,
hormones, oxy, ions,
fooling us as we fool around,
lab rats spellbound by
sorcery and science.

JACOB R. MOSES

Truffles

Hard shell, amorous ambrosia
Nectar, chocolate tastebuds
Sharing nomenclature with a
Luxurious fungus, aromatic
Psychedelic sensations rising
Kaleidoscopic third eye vision
Splash, senses stimulated
Like shocks emitted by a
Toaster in the Mediterranean
Feeling leaves me salty
Thirst now quenched
Fiend for the orgasm

JEREMY GADD

Cupid

Cupid does not let you choose
between the morally upright or slut
but, to my modern Theodora, am
I a Justinian or just another John?
Knowing she was/is promiscuous
with a proclivity not to stay,
who looks on love with disdain,
who usually leaves after she has lain;
who won't accept sexual boundaries
and finds most men limp or fey,
like Blake, I kiss the beauty as
she flies, hoping to bask
forever in Eternity's sunrise.

C. E. J. SIMONS

Tantalus

I thought when I was old that I'd grow weak.
Testosterone's stone fountain would run dry,
and wisdom, wisdom finally would speak—

forget the slippery curves, forget the sleek
transience of the fuck—the body's cry
for sex, more sex, more sex: for flexed obliques,

arched back, lips' rictus, tongue's long-learned techniques,
throat straining at the rush, the opiate high.
I thought when I was old that I'd grow weak—

muscles, and mind. But when your chest, your cheek
flushes with frank arousal, that's when my
wisdom speaks, and my wisdom finally speaks

clearly now, schooled by loveless nights gone by:
you thought when you were old that you'd be weak
but you were always weak, and you know why—

your wisdom doesn't grow, only your prick.
Your memory fades, but that hard flesh you try
to keep from ruining your life still piques

your interest more than books. YOU'RE GONNA DIE
it screams inside your head, STICK TO THE FREAK.
Testosterone's stone fountain may run dry,

but I'm in deep—neck-deep in a cold creek,
straining to drink, not understanding why
I thought when I was old that I'd be weak.

I knew what I'd become. I'm not unique.
Another dirty old man. I'd rather die
than ever be a man like that. So lie—
and wisdom, wisdom finally will speak:
it isn't weakness to love being this weak.

Making it Work with Medusa

Our snakeskin love's our unashamed
hiss at injustice. We've changed so much for each other—
but I'm often stunned I'm still the only lover
you haven't tried to change.

Our whole flat's mirrored, as per the risk
assessment. At bedtime you set two cucumber lenses
over your seaweed facial cleanse,
then strap on your welder's mask.

Sometimes during sex, I risk your basilisk-glare
and fire floods my retinas,
a sear that smolders
my prophylactic contact lenses' Mylar.

When you get up for work, you never forget
to lean across me and press
two fingers against my throat
to feel for a pulse—

then double-check there's a full bottle
of anti-venom on the night-table.
I hear your curls slither and fret
against your steel-mesh hair net.

In your studio, your dread locks
tied back, I thrill at your eye for still life—or better still
for human beauty hidden in a block
of marble.

We make ends meet, in this rich landlord's death trap.
When I'm depressed you cheer me up
with another exquisite sculpture of a rat.
You've promised to show the landlord the whole set—

and if he waves us off with some reply
about the rising cost of energy
you'll smile and set him straight, and then we'll see—
we'll see if he can look you in the eye.

TIM KAHL

Hot Hands

I pray to my foot massager. She comes to me
in my dreams at night. Without her a walk
over the crust of the earth in the daylight
is impossible. I fear I may never find her
in the public spaces where the other souls dwell.
I post a notice in the personals on Craig's List:
[Sacramento, CA] Oh, my little Hot Hands who
presses out the pain in my arches and makes it
radiate to my toes. I could feel our pulses fall
into sync together. Maybe this time we could
pretend it's real? Certainly it seems during
this pandemic I may have cracked my psyche.
My subconscious is leaking into the visible world.
But can I find her out there, the one who shares
our dream and knows me as The Squealer or
maybe as The Bearded Knuckle? If she could
only attend while I'm awake, I could say
my prayers were answered. Would she see me
as too American, lonely as a dropped feather?
Even a receiver of prayers can't be too impressed
if the query seems desperate. Will all my
longing counter this or just seem tawdry
after a while, like a dog tagging along after
its master. I obey you, but my feet obey
the laws of gravity. My feet move me through
the streets and meadows. Call me. Write me.
Send me e-mail. I need an appointment.
The catalog of touch is what makes me new.

The Temperament of the Nipples

They face adoption as doorknobs
and round buds of damaged saddle

They entertain the boss of light boredom and magic
with their emotion of happen-in-the-moment

Whether they can sense their own predicament
is a pained guess by those who know how to measure emptiness

Where do they store their food for the winter of sorrows?
How does red wine let them meet their commitments?

Their years in the regimen of clothes are applied
to the special treatment given during a tongue lashing

They imitate the modeling clay left out on the tree stump
They drag themselves across skin interrogated with a thumbnail

They put up with indecision, animal cries in the night
when they should be sleeping off a bold adventure

All day they live in their own worrying sweat
At twilight they awaken, a glamorous token of expected presence

So long in their padded domain, they are tired of being officiated
They wait for encouragement and stare steadily in amazement.

What kind of white do they turn in the absence of admirers?

The Kind of Shine

I too begin to sweetly cast a light
when you are stunned and naked awake
with all the strings of your lute
most recently played. In this state
of happy lunacy I turn to your face
and see all those hungry lines erased.
There is an ease that softens every
animal's fate in this moment,
and I am allowed to gaze into it,
add up the fortunate instants of
this grace. I am so proudly decorated
from these raids on your clever
existence . . . that you release into
magic lands. I am the wayfarer with
a wooden drum who returns home
to this place where the breaths come
and go like tidal beckonings. I want
to ask you (as does the sea)
where you find yourself wandering
when you take leave of the body's
underpinnings. Is it pinnacle or abyss?
Is there a light on that I must mirror
and shine back to you the kind of
shine that gently fills my eyes
and faithfully turns to shimmer?

PAUL ROWLAND

Missing Apostrophe
for Jean Cocteau

I
No matter how many elevators I ride
no angels speak to me. One day
will you step through the doors
and speak to me? Or
will you stand in silence,
shifting from foot to foot,
waiting for me to speak first?

II
Speak to me on the radio
in the static between stations,
repeating yourself like a bingo caller.
Speak to me and tell me your name—
will it be beautiful as his,
or something ordinary?
If you speak, I'll be your secretary.

III
I've never liked lifts:
we'll probably meet on an escalator
sliding in different directions,
or bump into each other in the street,
colliding like a kiss—but
how will I know it's you?

IV
Will you be wearing blue overalls
and wings of glass on your back?
Or will you be sporting a chauffeur's cap
on your black, immaculate hair?
Will you be male, or feminine?
Will you look like Bruno Ganz,
or someone that I used to know?
Will I be able to see you at all?

V

Maybe you'll come at an awkward moment,
when I'm having a shower or shaving;
maybe you've already been
but I was otherwise indisposed.
If you call by again, I'll be waiting.
Then again, maybe you won't
be a person at all, but
an orange.

Crossed Wires

Nothing is as it seems: my hair
is waving inside my head, neurons
blowing in the breeze, my veins
are river deltas and my nerves
winter trees on a distant hilltop.

There's more than meets the eye:
a crowd of photons clamoring
to shake tiny hands with my rods
and cones, to let my brain know
they are here from outer space.

I fling my arms up in despair
only to realize I'm dancing—or
waving for your attention—which
amounts to much the same thing.
Come and save me when you can.

DEBS MAX

Lost

I wrote a poem about sex on the way home but I lost it in the genkan,
dropping my house keys
juggling junk mail, bills, groceries…
You know you're most likely to forget things in doorways?

It was something about

      cicadas living underground for seven years bursting into light, bursting outta
      their skins, fresh-winged and screaming for sex like bros outta car windows
      HEY BABY HEEEY HEEEEY

and

      something about birdsong sounds so sweet and sonorous but in their hidden
      avian dialect it's just
      DICK! Hey I've got DICK! Baby hey DIICK! Come get some DIIICK

and

      something about the time I asked if I could lick a girl's tattoo, and the time
      I couldn't think of anything to say after 'hi' except "I've got those shoes" (I
      didn't)

and how lowkey sheer human awkwardness is to nature

But I forgot it in the genkan
 as the keys fell,
 the words slipped out
and slunk off into corners
      to roll around with the dropped
               oranges

Found

I knew the second I saw it, standing on charity shop tatty tired carpet in northern
England
This stone on the necklace was yours

I needn't touch it to know
this purple stone belongs to you
 steel-clad certainty, never been so sure of anything before
Though you've never seen it, you were born owning it
 long before the land I stand on had a name
it was yours

There's gentle mystery in idle speculation owners before,
and what they saw and where they went
or its real origins—was it crafted? Hewn? Molded? Forged?
Igneous Volcanic?
         Incandescent, those violet shapes formed in the violent heart of the Earth
 Sedimentary?
         Less dramatic, but—like the author—crushed by years and pressure,
         leaving lines in their gradual wake, like the limestone of my hometown
         great ancient corals displaced
         into moorland, now reaching up through purple heather to vast skies
Metamorphic?
         Ever changing, it needed heat and time to find its final form, patient and
         certain
                  some old souls still bear
                           fiery hearts

Above the pendant, a trinity of ovals encircled—
         power of threes   a spinning world
         Nordic   Celtic
          mythic   cryptic
—in the implicit spirituality of purple
         spectrum's edge   imperial
         king chakra   emperor

Admittedly slightly jealous to be the holder, not the owner
'destiny' too strong a word perhaps;
regardless, this isn't meant for me.

And all this hits in an instant
Still standing on tattered carpet over peat soil over limestone
while far outside the steel city
Peacefully austere, the lost coral swells right to the horizon over space too vast for
borders
          under August's purple heather
                    below the overwhelming sense of sky

GREG SNAZZ

A Hit

There was a pool and I jumped in.
Not to impress anybody but just cuz
I was fueled up. Wanted to get
naked. The Spanish couple clapped and
cheered me on. Hunger was scratching
its belly and yawning. Bone
necklaces. Leopard print everywhere.
Skipper caps. But the music was
hurtling forward, not going back.
Asian bands writing their own
Please Kill Me's. European bands
trying to keep up. So, I just
walked up and thought why not & said
aren't you off soon? Full of fuel
and maybe Venus was in retrograde.
Being the girl of someone's
dreams. I don't know if it's legal
to drink on the street in Ho Chi Minh
so I tested it. Crouching in the jungle
darkness with that French expat.
Had one too with a guy in a shop
selling beers from a cooler.
Couldn't speak English so we
just drank & smiled at each other.
Burlesque dancers. Tired-eyed
underground rock legends. Paisley.
Converse and skinny jeans and
big belt buckles and hair. A guy
leaped on a table but violence can't
get it up. Slick bartender serving drinks
that cost a fortune in local currency
to scuzzy rockers flush with dollars.
I said hey, you get off soon? He clocked
out quick. Look at that bold move.
Kim went partway, left us at the main
street. The second day, everyone paying
& refueling. Ate next to a

bike repair shop, the pho had hints
of gasoline. I slapped the sofa
and he sat. I loved that. I loved
the view from the roof of the venue.
All those tiny twinkling
lights.

Sexy Alien, Bowling Cosmic Strikes

sexy alien, bowling
cosmic strikes, lights
my terra nullius,
boogie-fires my
horny fuselage, revamps
unicorn age of
exploration, sneaks me
outta this planet
for romp that
melts iron

KEVIN CARTER

Alucinari

Hallucination is our solace
We are tantalized by desire's delusive elusiveness,
our full-fledged stares at unattainable grace
while shackled in a cozy cage of our own making
We daydream, then nightdream
Go insane to stay sane. Guerilla ontology
Our neurons regenerate within the cerebral cortex,
a projector flickering eyelid movies we don't want to end
I think DMT flows through us,
starry-eyed babies when we're born,
when we dream,
when we smoke,
and when we die
Oneiromantic Penrose fractals
we could never conceive of while Argus-eyed
Reality is cold and harsh
Instead let's buy surreal estate

REPATRIARE PERDITA

Pandora's Box

Given all that's left
Laid bare a doomed
    and tattered soul
White knuckled
     Clinging to the last remnants
False dignity to keep
    from Failing
    from Falling
    from Justifying notions of passion
    from Returning to acquiesced cold
co-dependency

Entreat me
Caress me
Charm me
With forked honeyed tongue
Seduce me

On me
   In me
     Around me
   Behind me
    Under me
    Over me
Inhale me
Exhale me
    Dissolve me
Scatter me

DECONSTRUCT ME
DESTROY ME
DIVIDE ME

Reconstruct me
  Rebuild me
    Repair me
      Make me whole

Cosmic

post-apocalyptic
high-speed pneumatic
try not to panic
       Stay—heart ecstatic
       drift on clouds Magellanic
bring it—said the romantic
kiss me there anti-climactic
forget the prophylactic
Hold it keep it breathe it tantric
I came breath post-orgasmic

we are binary stars co-sycophantic
our orbits are ecliptic
space intergalactic
I can die now dramatic
I die with you
but be pragmatic
celestial spaces are not deterministic
but interstellar stochastic

You and I are cosmic

My shopping list as his sub

*2 garter belts – 1 black; 1 white
   Make them match the camisoles.
*2 pairs thigh-high nylons
   It's okay if they don't match the
garter
   belts.
*2 bananas
*1 bag trail mix; no sunflower seeds
   That should be enough for you.
*1 case bottled water
   I can get more if you need it.
*1 box of band-aids – with round
   plasters preferably

*1 package razor blades
   Let's try not to make a mistake
   on this one again, okay?
   (Smiles and kisses back of
   her neck)
*1 ice pack large
*2 ice packs medium
*3 ice packs small
   Remember to put them in the
   freezer as soon as you get home.
**book spa day with Alessio and
   Bernadette
**book massage – ask for Trinh
   I'll try not to give you too many
   but they won't ask about the
   bruises. Tell them you're mine.

DUNCAN WHOM

Ground Zero

I.
an afternoon lull
so we slipped away,
unremarked
and in the stationery closet
hurriedly came,
upsetting a mop
getting our bodies back in clothes
among protuberant clattering utilitaria
is a fun of shrieking chaos collisions,
of worthy implements defying pleasure seekers
you leave first,
ducking into your cubicle,
and we nonchalantly resume our shift
but my fingertips
feel the keypads touching back
(because the lunchtime spliff)

the week pauses

by now I can hear through walls
zero comes
you refuse all eye contact
when there are others there
which is always in this office

but later we go to a vacant floor
and do it there

II.
everything is action:
wave upon wave
of tabi on tatami
shore laps tide
a ceramic wall leans
against a bamboo whisk
but without the glare of eyes

when the materials touch,
they are set at ritualized rest
(but when you folded the yukata
and your slender hand
lingered on the heaped silk,
I kissed the nape of your neck
and your blue black stubble
cut my lips)

oyu runs off a yielding spout:
waterfall to douse a cup warm,
a humble interlocking choreography
(but I prefer what you did in the *genkan*,
having just met me)

at length it arrives,
cloudy green and tepid,
with a tiny nub of pink sugar
(how to spend the evening after this?)
YES OK! 'perfect':
life; death; art; nature;
the extinction of ego
(too much balance can ruin an orgasm)
why are we in Kyoto? to fight?
No, I like tea scolding hot,
even green, steam coming off it,
with jazz hands and crenelations

kodomo mitai you say
yopparai

III.
and so
on carpet or mat
standing or laying
in closets in elevators
missionary on linoleum
with or without condoms
or emotional cum control
we've plateau-ed
and your veiled denying eyes
out cold

Delight [redacted]

Sunday January [withheld] 19[withheld]

His voice was different—grown I suppose—or also wounded.

But I liked how he [suggestive action] my [unnecessary detail] and [suggestive action]
with urgency.

I almost felt guilty that war had made our [inappropriate] darker but more delightful. I
wonder if he ventured there. We didn't talk much.

I let him place his [unmentionable]
in my [suggestive] [unmentionable] [inappropriately].

The afternoon passed in [inappropriate]
punctuated by sleep and [obscenity].

I watched him sleeping
knowing that within a day or two
he'd be back at the [confidential location].

I feel empty not knowing when or if we'll ever meet or maybe we'll both survive this and
[suggestive collocation] where we left off.

Sometimes I worry there's no hope beyond oblivion.

FARAH ALI

Ichijiku

watch him work on intricate tasks
remember when he drizzled honey
over a ripe fig prepared and presented
like a flower oozing warmth pouring
over each plump segment sweet
sticky fingers in your mouth

Shunga

My favorite Hokusai
is Kanagawa oki nami ura.
A convenient lie, as I much prefer
Tako to ama. Look at the pearl diver's
entanglement, how her thighs part,
swollen labia spread, eyes closed,
the ecstasy in her exquisite face,
her clutching, slender hands,
head thrown back
as those dread lips
bring her to the brink
again and again
and again.

Our Desire Is

Darker than a bruised limb,
Darker
       than a slit mouth,
Darker than a swarm of moth eyes,
Darker
       than a lamentation,
Darker than clotted blood,
Darker
       than yurei and yokai
Darker than a crow's broken wing
Darker
       than a stab wound,
Darker than annihilation,
Darker
       than a ring of death caps,
Darker than a kodoku jar,
Darker
       than ancient rituals,
Darker than Aokigahara,
Darker
       than torn membranes,
Darker than grief's desolation,
Oh, this dark
       Desire.

ALISON LUBAR

App[etite]

If you want
something
exotic, watch me
eat [your]
yakitori heart

A Canonical Haunting

at midnight, the hands of everyone
I've loved come grasping—fine, anemic
fingers of the piano playing pastor's son,

chipped black nail polish with power-
chord callouses, tobacco-
field tan, Sanskrit ink script billows above
aquamarine manicure.

I bite not nails, but knuckles
instead to taste copper-stigmata,
holy whorls and loops of every print

on my ribs, the gun of pointer-and-thumb
fumble to jugular with one hunger, wish:

my lungs close like a fist.

NORIKO MIZUTA
translated by Jordan A. Y. Smith

Unwritten Love Letters

While I'm standing here,
the wind brings tell,

the faint trembling of feathers,
a journey over the eons
insisting, further and further away,

countless unwritten love letters,

toward a place memory no longer reaches,
insisting, deeper and even deeper

Will the soul oblige and pause long enough
for them to catch up?
Will the soul rest a moment?
For someday they will catch up,

leaping across the abyss of oblivion,
insisting, even if they arrive too late,

love letters,
        countless,
                unwritten

RYAN DZELZKALNS

Landscape Without the Tamagawa
多摩川なしのランドスケープ

You can only see the sky from here.
　　ここから空だけ見える。

The embankment and its people without faces
　　堤防とその上の顔無しの人々は

block out everything else. Do you think
　　何もかもを塞いでいる。ねえ、雲が成功だ

the clouds have been successful? You can't tell
　　と思いますか？座っているところから

from where you're sitting, but everything is
　　分からないけれど見えている全ては暮れていて、

getting darker and pinker. There is so much grass
　　ピンクになっている。草がこんなに多くて、

and you can hear it all. The cars rumble past
　　その全てが聞こえる。コロコロと通っている車は

drowning out the bike's petite machinerie.
　　自転車のプティートマチンイリーをかき消している。

You stare at the sign with the cartoon who has a
　　頭に穴があるキャラが表れるサインを眺める。

hole in its head. Did he receive any warning?
　　彼は注意をもらいましたか？

From where you're sitting the trains hem you in
　　座っているところから、電車に縁取られていて、

and you can hear everything but the river.
　　全部が聞こえている、川以外。

The Bad Sons of Shizuoka

       Spouts of light scrape past Suruga Bay,
dapples proving that clouds rove across the dinted sea.

Breaking fast in a room of old people, we do not worry
       who will take care of our parents. See?

How the promontory that was dark is now cast in light?

SHŌZŌ TORII
translated by Taylor Mignon

Dazzling

through the glass window,
the moon sears transparent traces
on Mademoiselle V's burning back

a fully sound-proof room
enclosed by unseen containers

not yet, do it
harder

the blond beast's
sealed heart murmurs
and bends the ridge-line of her heavy breasts

from Mademoiselle V's black
gloves, the diamond whip cracking out a flash of death

at that time
the phantom ocean boils, casting off its mask

Weekend

Chasing pipe smoke
leaving for the twilight town of Clerici
petite fleurs that don't even try to do much of anything
O Aphrodite
because you're so excessively erotic
the door keys always shriek
holes inhabited by ancients
being infinitely mystical
are always covered with soft feelers
sound of pomegranates cracking open

Soft Fang

either that or
do you feel the black flames of a candle
and the whips of pleasure are bitter?
O Justine When a Cattleya orchid blooms
eternity's
night traveler dons a clay crown
tedious weekend
hugging a bible with missing pages
let's go to the erotic sea
together with the undead accomplices

SAMUEL LOUIS SPENCER

Ransom

The space on your neck, just below
and behind your ear and next to your nape,
makes your entire body squirm

both tense and limp, I cannot tell
who's hostage; for in one moment
I delicately sink my porcelain unto that place,
and the next you've a fist full of hair,
whispering: "Mine, mine, mine."

SARAH SANDS PHILLIPS

Blum and Poe Tokyo

Whatever comes after *hello*
we need an entire year of

Where we're not just staring at
each other, hoping the other will speak

Where I'm not, heel to toe, moving
around the room

looking at a painting I've already
loved three times

The First Time

do you think of me
when the
      night is out

or when daylight
  d r i p s
back into
     the room

do you imagine us
  drinking coffee the
next
morning

awkwardly cupping
  things
mugs
    our thoughts
      into

sentences into twisted
fingers
    fumbled into
again

ULYSES RAZO

Right Now I'm Pulling Apart a Tangerine, and Wherever and Whatever These Clouds Were Before They Were Here Feels Irrelevant in Light of My Having Now Realized That I'd Expected Something Better From the Sky

I hate the bur oak
beyond the library.

A rat gets dragged
by an axle and I

think that makes
perfect sense.

I take for granted
walks I'm on.

You taught me how
to take a picture.

I used to smile
with my teeth.

Wildfire

So it was
like a natural
disaster
I said.

You moved
your head.

Estuary

A cloud's moving a little too quickly today.

The metal in me waits
to be touched like a car
by a car.

I wish I wasn't tired of my sadness
and didn't think so much about
the distance between
I love you forever &
That love will never end.

A river and a tree are almost the same.
The latter drops its needles
into the former's mouth.

Did you make it can you hear her

ALEXANDRA FÖSSINGER

Changeling

To record   her body's history,
never entirely inhabitable,
to put fear in tiny boxes

has made her forget
the password   to life.

Preserve your soul
to make the bones rot alone,
someone told her.

All it was about, though, was

not to hear the ghostly noises
not to be a storage room.

Self

Thought that crosses the mind
warrior for time, pain keeper
matter once a year
word plucker, word giver,
something akin to a poem
treelike freelike
fearless prisoner
silence assembler
shy breather: listening, seeing
vessel on impulse and vocation
custodian of the holy,
always less beloved

a woman who has been waiting
for a hundred years,

and then nothing,
nothing.

ALEX WATSON

Pomegranate

In warm clay,
a tear-shoot branches
into a bloodshot flower.

A jewel of arils
flush with ruby water
tart, flaming.

Seized before its red rind wrinkles
leaving only its bite.

SRINJAY CHAKRAVARTI

Kalbaisakhi in the Sundarbans

the mirage-heavy shimmer
                of midsummer simmer.

coconut, palm, plantain trees
are frozen into still lifes.

                in the darkened bedroom
                of the overcast afternoon sky,

  the ceiling's cloudscape
  conjures up a gray sultry gloom.

        the wind gets fresh,
        and blows out the skirts

          of the washing hung out to dry
          on the clotheslines in the gardens.

the parched brown landscape is in heat.
its pants, breathless with anticipation.

                the crows and sparrows and mynahs,
                the mongrels and cats and cattle,

            all look up with bated breath
            for the first sweaty drop of rain.

    in the dreamscapes of her immersive sleep,
    she moves and moans and shifts her limbs—

        the foreplay of jagged streak lightning
        raising goosebumps on her skin:

            the electric alphabet
            of his amatory touch.

his febrile kisses ripple into thunder,

rumbling through all her erogenous zones.

    the puckered ridged nubs
    of her twin brown mounds

      become pointed, sharp, erect
      with slow, gentle arousal.
where the brackish river parts its thighs,
forked with creamy sandbanks,

    into a lush pubic delta—

    where a littoral tangle
    of dark secret *sundari* jungle

      is drenched in her briny perspiration
      and her sweet–tart sexual juices—

the Bay of Bengal seeps in, insinuating
itself into her very own hidden grotto.

    awakening, she holds this hush,
    this frissive hush, close

      to the drumbeats of her heart
      as they echo throughout her bloodstream.

      the hungry tide moves
        back and forth,
        back and forth,
its crest frothing with semen;

    till the thunderstorm breaks
    over her heaving, heavy breasts

and the sky ejaculates

      into rain,
      the orgasmic rain.

A *kalbaisakhi* is a violent pre-monsoon thunderstorm, common in eastern India and Bangladesh during April and May. The estuarine, swampy delta of the Sundarbans in the eastern Indian state of West Bengal and Bangladesh hosts the world's largest forest of mangroves, locally known as *sundari* ("beautiful trees").

EDWARD LEVINSON

Mystic's Lover

The mystics of old were right
to speak passionately of the Beloved
the Divine Presence
they tasted and strived to
know and embrace
even if they considered themselves
unworthy.

The true Beloved
the Divine Friend.

Mother Earth holds on to me
and I to Her
massaging each other
as we touch
knowing not who caresses whom.

Water in Her fluid forms
runs silky fingers
over my body
tickling my senses
beyond pleasure.

Sun penetrates me
but all I feel
is the soft bright light of a new day
or a final burning kiss
before it retreats into darkness.

Sweet Wind
feathers sweeping on my bare skin
in an inimitable way
unimaginable by human hands
stirring primal arousal.

Nature my lover
asking little giving much

the mystic embraces
partner's power
enchanted excited
energetic secret betrothal
hidden in his heart
infinitely entwined.

The mystics of old were right
to sing of their Beloved
with unashamed delight.

AL NINGEN

Satori For Two

Will I be born in the constellation of your arms
The deep space of your body
I have beheld a tender cosmos in your eyes
As I spin the straw of the day
Into the newborn sunshine of your smile
We have become the fabric of a universe you and I
Subtle as oxygen in blood
Vital as hydrogen
Two curious explorers
Of moments evolving from stardust and time
In everyday galaxies
Unknown to the rest of mankind
But familiar to us
We visit uncharted regions of the soul system
Past dead stars
To where new worlds have been created
By our own worlds' collision
Apparently singular
But randomly collective
We are borne to each other
Born of each other in the astral tide
The expanding universe of delight
Our transcendent smile
Vast and intimate
If ever I cause that smile to fade
Through faint heart or self-regard
To have travelled so
A million light years from home
Through entropic awe and darkness
To have reached out
And found beauty and desolation
Would be simple dharma
But to find joy no longer on your lips
Would be such a dark eclipse
And if you should take your bright star from my sky
Its extinction my evolution
Its light will last longer than I

And it will help me grow
Make me infinitely better
For what might be has at least been seen
Life rushed in
The vacuum became union
Before the planet tomb was sealed
Loving was revealed

The Physical World

Exploring the physical world
Kinetic synaesthetic être-en-soi
A ride where it's better to arrive than travel
And it's better to travel than arrive
On the hungry risingfalling
Achingsoothing oceanswell
Wanderlust unites and unties
The ascetic and the aesthetic path
Denial and sensation
The chain that frees and the freedom that binds
Discipline and excess
Mystery and history
Penetrates the honeyed moment
Straddles now
Tongues a different language
Sucks memory dry
Licks meaning from its lips

Where this is this is all there is

Jes Kalled, *Balcony* نسيت *(forgot)* أشجار *(trees)*

Brian Wood-Koiwa, *Body SUBconscious*

Vincent Aimée, *Espionage: Looking Back*

Vincent Aimée, *Osmosis: Assessment*

Sasha Drozd, *Burning Bush at Papaya, Love Goddess of the Cannibals*, 2022

Neil Craig Chapman, *Burning Bush*

Debs Max, *Self-Portrait*

Robert Holbrook, *Samushii*

Sanjay Bradford, *Alone In Ikebukuro City*

Ilias Tsagas, *Eretrian Boy, Torso*

The picture was taken in Greece's Archaeological Museum of Chalkis "Arethousa". The sculpture, dating 520–485 B.C., was unearthed at the Temple of Apollo Daphniforos in Eretria, Euboea Island, Greece.

May Drew, *Meghan*

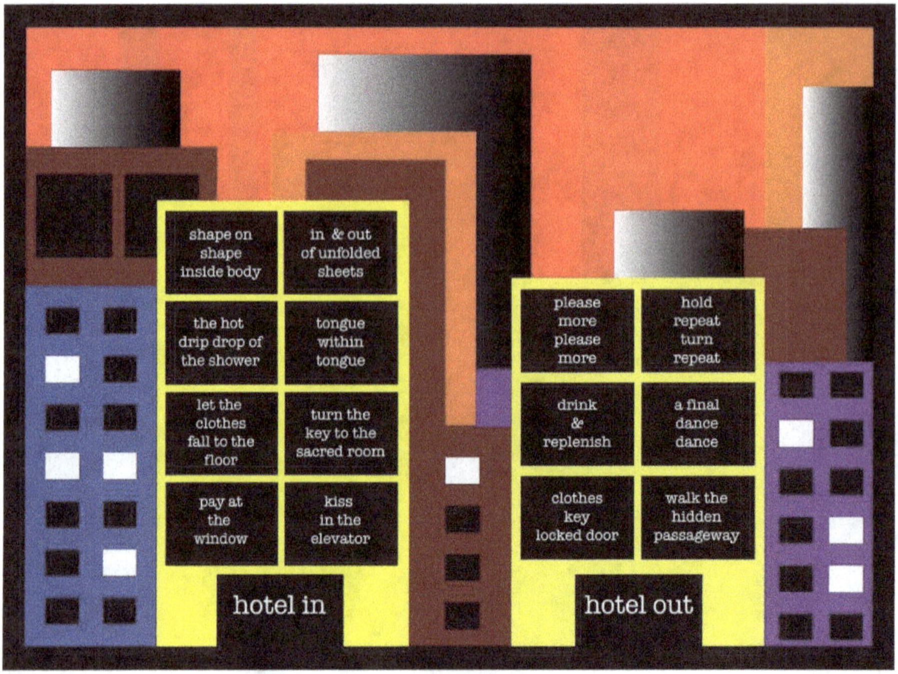

Herman Bartelen, *Hotel In, Hotel Out*

John Meyer, *Fire Angel*

Marcellus Nealy, *Untitled*

Peter Leghorn, *Beau-Monde*

YOWEN XAN

Yamato Boy

Koma 朝鮮 boy Kobe-kko 神戸っ子
Who pressed me chest to chest
And cheek to cheek
Belt undressed you'd come undone 「こっち」
Boy undone such ease
He uncovered himself
Smothered himself under me
Covered himself with my body
Swaddled himself in my black skin
To escape the hate of what he is
Yamato boy
Who pressed me chest to chest
And cheek to cheek
Lay with me flesh to flesh
Inbreathed my breath
To the depths 「ああ、チョアっ」
Koma boy Kobe accent
Back and neck to neck kiss the nape lips naked,
Legs entwined hand to breast your face
Poured out my sweat and drenched you fingers laced
Eyes gazing eyes glazed pulse racing
Left you wet and drenched you panting spent you'd shuddered often
Lost, your mind beset with old thoughts
My mind besotted with silent thoughts of you

DATIKO

It Didn't Seem to Want Us

That night years ago
Fucking that girl
Against the metal railing
Atop the upper tier
of the Eiffel Tower
In her white two-piece
Holding her wrists
which she had willfully volunteered
Above her head
As I feverishly whispered in her ear
right hand on her willing hip
Of the heat and pleasure of a lusting couple
She was moist with heat
at the tantalizing temptation
of transgression
of imagination
in knowing that I knew
that she wanted
what I wanted
as much
as she
secretly
before a crowd of our peers
Leering drunkenly
and chattering gayly

Oddly,
although we both knew what we wanted
it didn't seem to want us
as we quietly discovered later

That was the Parisian summer
Of frenzied teenage fornication
Five frenetic encounters

Yet only two days later
she was

Anonymously sexually assaulted
In the most egregious manner
on the Paris Metro
...grounds for disembowelment...
before a colorful noisy crowd
Leering and chattering

these things happened

the rush,
denouement
and transgression
of Lust...

Bare Japanese Feet

She let me touch
at the breakfast nook
One morning

Never mind the nail

MIHIRO OGAWA

Being a Satyr, Momentarily

I hope there is such a thing as endless lovemaking.
    The pleasure of sex lasts only a tiny bit of time.
    How good it would be if this would last until I die!

This could be scary, too, because having sex without stopping
    makes a man a satyr.
      If a man becomes a satyr,
      he must surround himself with nymphos.
      This sounds euphoric,
      but he must bang each nympho every night
      so as not to anger her
      and make her leave him.
      This utopia can turn into dystopia
      at any given moment.

This thought is what anyone has while they are making love
    but forgets when they are doing anything else.
    The time of my existence here on the earth is contemptible
    in comparison to the unimaginable time in which the universe
    has been existing since it was created 13.8 billion years ago.
    The time of my having sex is nothing,
      completely invisible.

The thought of eternal lovemaking is too radical.
    It may be enough to bang someone sometimes.
    But when he fucks, he craves it more.
    Oh, man, better to finish it up soon,
    since it is only a tiny spoonful of pleasure
    of being a satyr
    to trigger
      a flood of dopamine
      in his brain
    at just one moment
    of dozens of minutes
    of his whole life
    on this earth
    within this universe.

Jordan A. Y. Smith

「走れエロス：Run,
Eros, Run!」

夜遅く
ロウソクと言葉
都会のどこか
多分　喉が
乾く　瞬間
出版した本が
詩から物販
になった
悪循環
１１０％果汁２００％
怪獣
毎週、大衆が群れる眠
れる美女と野獣スキー
場で野球
合わへんやろう
　　　　Thank you
　　気にせんといて
ビキニを捨てて海に出よ
だめか　だめか
なぜか　なぜか
狼なくせに
全然
吠えないのか
あッ、分かった
吠えるのが怖いのか
まあ、いいやん
いつか　鉢は
はちみつを作るように
ならんと　ならん
definitely
もうニコニコしすぎた
顔の筋肉を脱ぎた
　　くなった、
　　But you don't say FUCK NO
　　to Chuck Norris, do ya, Becky?
吸血鬼のエネルギ
吸い取られる血液
頭脳につけた
知恵の点滴

Latenight
Language with candles
Somewhere in the city
Maybe the moment
A throat dries out
The published volume
Turns from
Poem to commodity
Vicious cycle
110% fruit juice
200% monster
The public flocks weekly
Sleeping beauty and a beast
Baseball on ski slopes—
Bad matches
Muchas gracias
Pay no mind
Toss bikini for ocean protest
No good? No good?
Why so? Why so?
You're a goddamn wolf
but we can't
get a howl?
Ah, I get it—
It's too scary to howl
Forget it
Someday you'll have to change—
Every bee
Makes its honey someday
claro
Grinning overdoses
Wanna slip right out of these
Tired facial muscles

Vampiric energies
Blood sucked out
Wisdom IV drip
Brain-connected

免許も免疫なし　　　　　　　No license, no immunity
暑い、暑い　　　　　　　　　This heat, this heat
膨大なる面積に　　　　　　　Peregrinating around
遍歴する　　　　　　　　　　Vast acres of surface
演劇　　　　　　　　　　　　Theater
ぜひ　　　　　　　　　　　　Please
　　　　　Let me get sexy
平凡な革命へ弔辞を送る　　　Lift aloft a dirge for some average revolution
哲学じゃねぇぞ　　　　　　　It's not fucking philosophy
緊縛　失格　　　　　　　　　Bondage　　　Disqualified
失敗、失業、　　　　　　　　Failure　　　Unemployment
I'm sorry—
　　この漢字をどう読むんだっけ？　　　　How do you read this kanji?
　「失恋」＝　しつれん　や　しつこい　　Is it *shitsuren* (love lost)
　　　　だったけ？　　　　　　　　　　or *shitukoi* (tenacity)?
二回：twice, with dice
大好き　大好き　　　　　　　I love you　　　I love you
I scream for ice cream
結構　　　　　　　　　　　　　　　　　No thanks
let's go　　　fuck　　each other's brains out—
totally retro.
絶頂、絶頂　　　　　　　　　Climax　　climax
一回だけ：絶好　　　　　　　Just once: ideal
Petroleum fogs:
who let the dogs out?
who let the gunmen in?
who popped the cogs out
tropic of clockwork orange?
sun so bright, shine light at the right time
but none of it's mine
In sum: I love the nighttime
星は　天空で　停電し　　　　Stellar power outage in the heavens
ダイヤモンドは永遠に　　　　Diamonds forever
夜空に永遠の ZERO　　　　　Eternal nightsky: a ZERO bomber
基点となる０年に　　　　　　In the originary Year 0
めろめろの Hello—　　　　　Mushy hellos—
命令の迷路、　　　　　　　　In a labyrinth of commands,
走れエロス、走れ！　　　　　*Run, Eros, run!*

王・エクス・マキナ
"Rex ex machina: Global Villains Libretto II"

**

Overture[s] :

王・エクス・マキナ
Rex ex machina
Stopping the action
Taxing the ex lax
王
Rex *backs fashion*
with sex packets
bracket the aesthetic
let's just get it
  copacetic petting
   erases debts if you let it

Epichivalric Duet in B[positive]:

    if you be my simian

    I'll be your hominid (honey)

  I'll be your oblivion
  if you be my carotid
    I'll be your homicide

    if you'll hire me after

  I'll be your Quixote *bona fide*
   if you'll squire me master
    if you'll inspire my laughter

    I'll guffaw you out to breakfast

   I'll kiss your ebay
  if you'll suck my funky craigslist
    if you'll be my exit

    from *stare-hard-retard* scars

  I'll be your suspension bridge
  from the inferno to the stars

Prologos[Villain]:

王
  and in stepped **Rex**
エクス・マキナ
 ex machina decked
in tricolor festoonery

85

mustache and stacked pecs
spectacles flecked
with genetic chains
without a shred of EVIDENCE
that anything is gonna change
狂 let's prearrange the whole
affair and wash hands of it
狂 forward the prenup with
fineprint in Sanskrit
狂 attach it to an anklet
anchored in Java Trench
and a broken pencil requiring
VISA and PASSPORT to rent
    C'MERE, WENCH, ARGH.
      SHARE A TURKEY LEG WITH ME
        LET YOUR BEAVER CHEW MY PEGLEG
      INTO A HIGH SEAS LEGACY
    IT'S ONE HELLUVA DELICACY
tell me, honestly now
    did you think Jack would refuse
        the magic beans to keep the cow?
          now iPlow fields, baby
            iReap what iSow
              when those dragon teeth
          iPlanted last spring begin to grow
        who knows? might just sell
      the whole outfit for an arm
      and a leg, cause most folks beg
      for their chance to buy the farm
      iDances with charm

      and wolves and pizzazz
on sabbatical relax mode
PLUS MECHANICAL JAZZ
these fanatical has-beens
iLove 'em to leave
but gotta please VOTERS
so iBloat 'em with cheese

    PLEASE, PASS THE *ass* MAN

      TANK'S ON 'E'
      PLEASE PASS THE MANNERS MAN
    THANKS TO *ME* イイイ*!*

Refrain of the Primo Uomo:

王・エクス・マキナ
Rex ex machina
rock-in-a-sock-in' ya

iPut the ass in the class and

hip hop in the opera
nobody's shopping
for alternatives
just testifying with
praise and superlatives

First Aria of the Behemoth Homunculus:

Oh, oh, oh, bustit—   エム・シー・ハンマー。
iSTEP ON THE SCENE
    LIKE LEAN CUISINE
        TO NOURISH THE HUNGRY BODY
    AFTER FITNESS ROUTINES
I've witnessed the screams
And the pulling of hair
王・エクス・マキナ
Rex ex machina mania
Permeating the air
A careless and reckless
type of au de cologne
with microphone essence
Alpha Male pheromones
iWear it at home
        iSpray it on you
                iSpritz it on the BUSINESS
                        That we're daring to do
So on the didgeridoo
Tambourine and kazoo
王
On the cymbals, **Rex**, a symbol
Of the hullabaloo
        The dulling of hues is

        hereby banned in my land

I'm asking for your *asses*

While I'm kissing your hands
    PEOPLE MISSING ME PACK
        THE POST-KATRINA SUPERDOME
        GETTING GIDDY WITH THEIR TITTIES

87

ON THE VIDEÓPHONE
iReally don't own 'em
And they're free as can be
But they fling their undergarments
And their souls at me
Though I'm sup*pos*ed to be
Like a MEGAPRODUCER
iBeg another egg
From the RUTHLESS in stupor
So toothless Mr. Hooper
Won't sell me the apple
Just the sauce, BUT I'M THE BOSS
   PEOPLE CRACK WHEN I TACKLE
     PUT THE SNAP IN THE CRACKLE
   AND PUT THE POP IN YOUR SMILE
I haven't stopped in a while
So let me flop on this pile
That's so soft that my style
Hits the pillow and sleeps
While my feet carouse the street
    Like: *I'm just keeping it deep*

Refrain of the Primo Uomo:

王 ・ エ ク ス ・ マ キ ナ
Rex ex machina
Stopping the action
Rocking the plaid slacks
Rex *backs fashion*
with sex packets
bracket the aesthetic
let's just get it
copacetic petting
erases debts if you let it
王 ・ エ ク ス ・ マ キ ナ
Rex ex machina　　　　　　　　王・エクス・マキナ
rock-in-a-sock-in' ya

I put the ass in class and

hip hop in the opera
nobody's shopping
for alternatives
just testifying with
praise and superlatives

Second Aria ^{a la schizophrenic}:

88

<ruby>Rex ex machina<rt>王・エクス・マキナ</rt></ruby>

rock-in-a-sock

whirling dervish

furnishing 360 cockblock

GOTTA ROCKET CROTCH.

SOMEONE GOT A POCKETWATCH?

clock the turbo-boosted juice

loosed on fools stopping to jock it

let's rock it like Davy Crockett,

KING of the wild frontier

a moment of violence

fer the buckskin pioneer   [GIVE 'EM WHAT-FER, DAVY!]

I'm tryin to hear the disco

but the party is live

    I babble with the rabble

      Babelfish for the jive

        wishing for wives

cause I'm a man o' the bed

with a plan to free the damned

from the land of the dead

put a brand on their heads,

uniforms on the ranks,

spanking bottoms if I caught 'em

not giving me **thanks**

bust a prank—oo ン!—you're shanked

<ruby>don't touch my moustache, indeed<rt>ド・ウ・イ・タ・シ・マ・シ・テ</rt></ruby>

seeking sympathy from me's like

teaching turnips to bleed

I don't need your *assistance*   アイス・ティー

I just need your *ass*

then I go the whole distance

and I go it with class

    ...by the vats

Epichivalric Duet 2.0 in B^{negative}:

—I'm <ruby>Rex ex machina<rt>王・エクス・マキナ</rt></ruby>—

王・エクス・マキナ

I'll be your Valentine

    If you'll suck my Israel

I'll lick your funky Palestine

I'll be your palace swine
you'll be my pigsty diamond
You'll by my Little Bo Peep

and I'll be your Simple Simon

if you'll be my dimple smiling
I'll lasso the sun
and give him titty-twisters
till he admits you're number one
sister

メチャイタイヨー。

[THE PLAY'S THE THING,
WHEREIN THIS CONSCIENCE HAS NO KING]

AHAHA! DON'T TOUCH MY MOUSTACHE! etc.

NISHALYA

Fruited overture

I watch you as you spread
the halves of the pomegranate
apart, its skins resting on your palms,
its inside juices coating your fingers.
You tell me it's sweet as you lick
the dripping syrup off your wrist, your hand
that stays a second longer in between
your lips, sounding out for you the sigh
stuck behind your gritted teeth. You pull apart
the best seeds, the most plump and succulent
ones, and give them to me
with your glazed smile,
teeth still playing with a once exploding seed
as I confess
amidst your mouthfuls
of tart maroon,
a million moons of ardor and I
would strip off all that good girl upbringing
for a single death
as that fruit in your hands.

HERMAN BARTELEN

As Nakedness Descends

as nakedness descends
with tongue on neck
spine skin & nail

as my hand
reaches into the
opening of her robe

breasts
first the left
then the right

slowly
curving past a thigh
my hand dips

into wetness
petals in bloom

The Spell of (Jealousy)

jammed and thrust into	(doubt)
errant eroticism	(delayed)
asinine & hard	(ardent)
licked and lustful, stalled	(in flames)
obstruction – frustration	(fiction)
unreal astatic unhinged	(irrational)
sex & suggestion in hues of	(insignificance)
thirsting always for	___________
	(you)

ZORIA PETKOSKA KALAJDJIEVA

[cyberotica]

Wired in Shibari
Tokyo electric pole dance
Hard on at HARD OFF

"again."

Wired in Shibari

|

Tokyo

.

Electric

.

Pole

.

Dance

.

Hard on at HARD OFF

.

JONATHAN PESSANT

Vaporware

I mean it's like Japan in the 80s up in here—excessive, extravagant restraint. Our naked city spills just the right amount of post techno-climate-feminist theory, like soggy bread crumbs rehydrated for peach-fuzz fanatics. We get hit! In our stereo beat reproductive organs. But Nuahsor and I, we all ready for the isms. The neo-auto-erotic capitalisms, the way-too-out-there- Ponzi-enabled liberalisms, the long-dead-yet-somehow-resurrected-and-always-talked-about-with-a-wave-of-the-hand landmine enthusiasms. Yeah, feels like prison sheets. Automatic and automatically caressing the folds out our streets, the streets with the treats and angel-faced peeps. There's a bar underground us, a barrier between this and that, the staunch stench of human living and the E-womb. Cell block life. I mean all the apartments are bars, round-thick and wide, enough to stick it in peep-show eyes. Nuahsor and I live here. She and me cohabitate. We don't make babies; it's passé. A hardcore sin. Who'd want to survive in this shit anyway. There's a hurricane coming, a whopper they say. Damn! Me and her just made it through the last-ditch-effort-swallowed-sinkhole brink. Last week, fires. Last month, two cities abandoned, underwater. We hear beech trees screaming. Everywhere I close my eyes, blurring. I can hear the future gurgling. It sounds like dial-up, unnatural and anticipatory. Like gills, man. Heavy breathing, bitter-skipping across broken concrete lakes. Nuahsor believes we're gonna die tomorrow. I kinda agree, kinda relieved.

20 Minutes from Asakusa to Daimon Station

Huh! There's no real etiquette   for sweating through your shirt
      in front of dozens of strangers   on a train to the temple
        you want to pray in.

Tokyo in September is like
      Boston after the 4th,
        utterly barbaric heat,
but goddamn the subways
      on the JR line, ice cold.

I stand, though there's scattered seats available:
      one by a tardy salaryman
        pseudo-manspreading,
          not enough to be American,

      two by an elderly obaasan,
        her face as youthful as her
          daughter and granddaughter,

        one more by three teens switching
          between English and German.

There must be a local festival near Nihombashi,
      thin bodies rush out,
        seats clear. I sit
        a little drier
          a little less like Beantown.

Two feet root themselves in front of me,
      nails painted plum
        a big toe winking at me
          in Louboutin sandals.

      Is it proper for me   to be
        so close
        our knees
        strike up
        conversation?

From her Gucci Ophidia bag she draws   a black wide-toothed comb and compact

straightens her straight black bangs   her hips willow with the track's clack clack clack.

Observing herself in the tinted mirror-window behind me   she powders

etiquette to her cheeks, jawline, the warm triangle where neck meets shirt button.

        Why doesn't she sit down?

                        I want her to stay,

                                    our knees are laughing.

JOY WALLER

Love Hotel Sketches: Osaka

He stands naked
in front of a cracked
mirror, shaving

That hypnotic scrape
of razor on exposed neck

Last night's cigarette smoke
and bergamot cologne
still fragile on the sheets

Love Hotel Sketches: Kanazakura

Topaz-tinted
October

       wind
       storm

       late-night coffee
       & chill-wave

You & I transport
banana bread
all the way
from my kitchen
in Tokyo
to a pink-lit
establishment
in Yamanashi
called The Washington

       chandeliers
       gold wallpaper
       marble floors

       located between
       a rice paddy
       and the highway

I take your camping
knife, cut moody slices
strewn with chocolate & walnuts

Serve them
on a chipped
white saucer
meant for tea cups

You grind coffee
beans by hand, boil

water in the portable kettle

Pour it gently
into glass cups
from the mini bar

      dining like this!
      drinking like this!

Curled up
on the faux
leather sofa,
giant crystal
ash tray
on my knees,
your American
Spirits & matches

      roosters outside
      big trucks &
      highway buses

And you & I

sex-drenched

breakfasting
at the Washington
as though we
are senators

Love Hotel Sketches: Uguisudani

When I pull
aside the woolen curtain
at dawn I see that
the window overlooks
a vast inner-city graveyard

The man shaving
at the cracked mirror and sink
across the room
is 16 years my senior—
he'd said good morning
by gently slipping
his tongue
between my legs

("It was the only way to wake you up"
          —a shy smile)

"How symbolic is *this*!" I yell,
gesturing with my cigarette
at the tombstones

(I'm maybe still drunk?)

He hesitates,
the razor delicate
in the fingers of one hand,
eyes torn between
his reflection in the mirror
and the view
beyond the window

(He's maybe already
becoming a symbol?)

It would be nice
to stay longer but
check-out time
is at 6

Love Hotel Sketches: Asahi

cerulean
   midnight

one slice
   of 7-11 cheesecake

two plastic forks

a look

wrists pinned
    to delicate
        cherry wood
          bed frame

a tongue
   sliding
      slowly
        down
          a rib cage

cigarette-lit
   afterglow

pacific ocean
   crashing
      and thrashing
        by the window

two troubled hearts
   beating neon
      in the middle
        of nowhere

MICHAEL ELY

Jazz Bar

Slow notes rising
And the shadow of your hand
Against his face

ALICIA ELKORT

Malibu, Evening Pool Party

The warm jasmine winds across a lanterned pool.

Faces adrift in moonlight.

Dark ocean across a mountain range.

I now recognize the moment I was able to praise beauty,
no longer a need for the object of praise to be me,
just resplendence on any ordinary night.

The dress—a large silk scarf, mustard with forest green.

I don't recall whether there were flowers or circles, a small shape, anyway.

Her long brown hair anchored behind her back to lift a glass and take a sip,
then her smile, the soft eros of youth.

I never saw her again—she couldn't have been more than twenty.

I drove home through the canyon and knew something had shifted.

A new territory.

ANDREW GEBERT

Ode to the couple who took my virginity

I was sixteen
she was in my
writing group
she and her old man,
as people said
in those days,
were in their thirties.
We were
hanging at her house
smoking and drinking on
August 8, 1974
the night Nixon resigned.
We celebrated with
a game of strip poker
and one thing led to another.

I was with her for a while.
She was soft and full.
I think she got off.
Then she turned
over and away.
She later told me
this was because
she thought the real action
was between me and him.
And she was right
I finished with him.

After that
I saw him a few times
at his cabin
in the woods.

Once, I was with
the mother of a friend
who was something
of another mother to me.

It was 10 p.m. and I told her
I had somewhere I needed to go,
could she give me a ride?
She drove me up
to the cabin in the woods,
dropped me off
without comment or question
for my "assignation"—
the word another harvest
from the writers group.

He had an impressive
collection of 1930s Bakelite pieces
which really do seem to
glow from within.

After I came once,
he fried some eggs
and I came again.
He murmured his praise
of being young
and eating yolks.

He said I was welcome
whenever I wanted
to come by
but whatever it was
faded with a little time.

Later, she brought a piece
to the writing group
about his violence.
I wrote a piece
from his perspective
called "Early Plastic."

At some point I heard
he had been
using heavily
and had a stroke.

There was nothing
transporting or seismic
about any of it.
But I was happy
to cross this off the list
to get this one thing done
in my fevered pursuit
of becoming adult.

BILL HOWELL

Later Than Us

Enormous shadow flakes sift past
streetlight indifference, adding us up.

Having been fallen out of love with,
we round out the edges, sinking

into now. If we were snow, we'd go
softer & slower. And just get the drift.

If absence can be inconspicuous,
silence is its willing accomplice.

DAVID CHENERY

Ghost Chain

I can show you
    the Dance of Death
Eyes aglaze with mouth foaming
    Screaming

Incantations to summon ghosts
in black obsidian verses

    dragged by somnambulance
into the sulphurfires of Summer

It dulls the knife
and sharpens the melodies
in a cage of memory

SORCHA CHISOLM

Dirty Hair

Dirty hair on my pillow
Gotta wash it clean before tomorrow
Dirty hair that touched your shoulder
Less than 24 hours and it was over

In your car you drive it fast now
Gotta suck it up cause it won't last now
I got an itch I need to scratch
Against my box light your match

Salt lingers on the air and on my tongue
Morning had come and we'd just begun
Breathing your breath was the hardest part
Not walking away

Dirty girl fix your mask now
No one will know if they don't ask now
You and me we've got this secret
The blood has flowed so the moon won't leak it

Dirty hair on my pillow gotta wash it clean before tomorrow
After all it was just a man who'd been there
It's not as if I haven't sinned yeah
　Wash it away

(You can listen to "Dirty Hair" here.)

SIMON SCOTT

The Bento Box of Tokyo

I see Tokyo as a Monday morning bento
eaten by a balding, suited salaryman on a bench in Hibiya Park.
Soy sauce dripping down his chin,
as the orange ash of lightly grilled salmon flakes flutter
onto pants grey.
Mondays are just like this. Separated into compartments,
only a teaspoon of potato salad, too much cold rice and no beer.
Then it's solitary coughs in public toilets, prayers in empty shrines and masks again.

Over medicated micro-discs of electric yellow daikon hummm
and their foil wrappers they flicker
like downed UFOs
in old 80s sci-fi movies.
Pointing, without prejudice, to the metaphysical potential of the solitary salmon slice,
and the pussy pink of unfulfilled Akihabara sex shop masturbation madness.

The weekend hangs heavy
like the sinful puff pastries of Shimbashi office girls' sugary indulgences
returned to the awakened eye which eyes
the mitochondria of bare takoyaki ball sacks enjambed
in butt cheeks dripping sauces dark brown
and teary eyed as tonkatsu sandwiches
(who the fuck thought of that?)

While Picasso paints the still life of a fat Xmas ham
and grandfather's carving knife cuts to perfection,
succulent slices of my life fly by uneaten
delicious globular chunks dipped
in Costco sized dollops of vinegary yellow mustard.
Stop for nothing now the applesauce legs of Tuesday tipping.
The Hatsudai Hub is a golden mecca of pre-corona fish n' chips
bubbling in the cooking oil of All Tomorrow's Parties
with Ricardo the Kiwi crim who talks to walls
while the masked nervous waitresses bow to Tokyo;
and sinister sailors are beached onshore
by frothy wild waves of Kirin-Ichiban
to live out their lives on an archipelago of badly baked miniscule shepherd's pies

with gawking middle-aged Pilipino wives.
What is wrong with it, I say? Cut the pie and see how the pieces fall... To death, be
damned.

I am a custard pudding, lime chuhai supping hunk of New Zealand meat,
lamb for the barbie, devil be spared.
We drag our crying bodies to the top of the mount...
Fuji-san, famous for sansai nabe which makes you take very, very stinky water shits in a
hurry,
beckons...
I leave the path of Aoki-gahara suicide forest sea of trees
floating in primordial swamp
I hear the voices of the dead cry
tears of terror in the chilly vegetable dawn,
where nothing grows
but the plastic bento brains
of well fried chickens.

Twiddle Twaddle

The ol' crapola bulldust brain fog flappa-doodles
premonitions of early death
in the terminal terminal
of BUSTA, bust a motherfucking fucker's jaw, bus station
shit show Shinjuku creeps weeps
drip dribbling malarkey
odorous as offal bubbling
glop slop swilling
bad beer and chewy squid
Under an ill, murderous sun
the democracy of death permeates.

A brain swells dangerously inside its cradle,
babies cry in abject fear of pure life death realization
and I see you already
your bony long fingers flickering
in evening light.
Bling blang lil' gimme girl with oh, so soft white skin
It bash in my skull and the dribble rot wash
over our saintly bodies
ice cream sodas just for two
(*May I lick the tears slowly from your face?*)
then a departure
by sea.

So, give me bulldust!
Golden dawns of bulldust
that are freed like words
from the bunkum of grammar
and university back alley backdoor action to didactic death
To taste again the sweet apple sauce of the senses
while shoeless cobblers drink whiskey cobblers
and long-legged cocktail waitresses run
skinny neo-capitalist Tokyo time.
(*On a mosey temple Sunday I feel free*)

Free ya flapdoodle blathers and wack on and off a good bushwa in the toffee
Book under his arm, *Havers Codology*— the perfect read for the bus
while staring at the flash of white

of her gentle neck, in gear now, all aboard, bento boxes of eyewash gibberish
All in, all codswalop and bilge bosh bull bunk
Hoot! Hoot!
Enough! Sip ya beer and poppycock ya cock
ping pong pocket pussies, glide
forever smoking Shinjuku Sunday behind us
Let us hog tie the driver, go on a killing spree and die in love
Good looking and cinematic
Phooey hooey tears drop on the bus floor
and lovers make slow jive
down in the foggy alleys of the end of Edo
where Okayama onsen picture postcards speak
Suicide death by cloudy water
and life a bent cuckold cock
crossing thru
the long circle jerk of time.

PHILIPPE BÜRGIN

Ginsberg Variations

1st
One summer's night's depths: Smolder, smolder, oh, smolder...
Sweaty breeze of innocent hearts—too young for this joke
about Saint Isidore of Montevideo, patron of patricide,
whose martyrdom was asking for mercy without avail:
"How do you plead, son?" asked the judge...
"Not guilty," pled young Isidore, "so please let me go,
your honor, there's already enough on my plate,
you see, I have a funeral to prepare,
I have just lost my father..."

2nd
A betwixt love, hysterical & hyperbolic, ensued,
with "the evening [...] spread out against the sky
like a patient etherized upon a table",
a dissecting table, in fact, ready to conduct
a vivisection with a sewing machine—
"Sharper than a scalpel to a patient
to an open heart, it's a daily operation"
of seams and ink, one soul, two beats,
out of sync, once the grain split &
one had to be left alone in the rain...

The lover's umbrella, left on the dissecting table,
found a second life as a corset, but only until
the fairest cocotte of all of Paname suffocated
betwixt its tight seams... As the scripture has it,
she said upon her last breath: "Do not call me Naomi;
call me Mara, for the Almighty has dealt very bitterly with me" (Ruth 1:20).
It's just one of these angry fixes of ghetto humor
for which this side of town is so famous for &
therefore, I stand here, speaking a prayer in honor—
of each and every one whom the Almighty has dealt bitterly...

And isn't it bitter? That moment when we have to admit
the fallibility of our Lord Father and the Holy Mother,
yes, they have never really thought of the names of their offspring,

like their parents before them and theirs before them...

3rd
It might be a sentimentalist's fancy to quote other poets,
far more refined and accomplished than they might ever be,
but there is truth to Rilke's verses: "beauty is nothing
but beginning of Terror we're still just able to bear,
and why we adore it so is because it serenely
disdains to destroy us."

But, is there anyone who may listen to such an elegy,
yes, anyone to whom the phrase *Ein jeder Engel ist schrecklich*!
means so much more than "Each single angel is terrifying"?
How terrifying, one might have asked & the answer circles around:
Mal de Cœur, Mal de Siècle & Mal d'Aurore

"If my complaints could passions move," thus wondered
limping, scraggy Mouche, worn-out by a brave little tailor,
munching down clam chowder boiled in her mother's milk—
she barely found refuge in the Basilica of Sacré Cour:
SACRATISSIMO CORDI JESU, GALLIA PŒNITENS ET DEVOTA ET GRATA,
a promise of salvation crumbling under a hail, hail, hail of bombs...
The tesserae of the confectioner's mosaic fell into gravel,
from gravel to gravel...

4th
A somber piano, an old tune, on a ship to a new world:
Bei mir bistu shejn, bei mir hostu hejn, bei mir bistu ejner ojf der welt...
"I came to this world to deluge you in flowers," the little tailor told the neophyte.
"For this and nothing else I came into this world."
"Would you give your eyeteeth for that?" she asked him.
He responded: "All of that and so much more..."
Thus, she spoke: "No bouquet will ever take my bitterness from your tongue."

5th
On the other table sat a Rabbi with his secretary: "Herr Rabbi," said his secretary,
"I notice you're reading *Der Stürmer*! I can't understand why. A propaganda sheet!
Are you some kind of masochist, or, God forbid, even absorbed by self-hatred?"
"On the contrary, Madame Secretary. When I used to read the Jewish papers,
all I learned about were: Pogroms, Riots, Assimilation. But now that I read this...
Oh joy, I see so much more: that we control all the banks, that we dominate in the arts,

and that we're on the verge of taking over the entire world.
You know—it makes me feel a whole lot better!"

6th
There are sometimes footnotes to stories, but why
aren't there also "clubfootnotes"? Which is to say,
what do we make out of these additions that never
get a foothold in the stream of consciousness, that never
find a footing, that miss to put the best foot down and forward...
So, the question remains: How may we speak of the sighting
of our ancestors, of those who couldn't foot their bills,
who were swept off their feet, who lost the ground
under their feet and landed six feet under...
How may we tell of said martyrdom that started
With the well-meant footnote: "Break a leg!"?

7th
Many have drowned in the *Reibach* & nobody knows: Goyish or Yiddish—
the soil doesn't care who's lying in the coffin, only the occupier cares,
From hail to hail to hail there was no rest...
Not even behind the Great Pond, not even in their dreams
where on each morning they would find a bouquet next to their bed
"Picked to be beautiful with me & to be loved for this mere reason," whispered the nun.

8th
To the roots, buckled, twisting and distorted, but never aligned...
Except "once in a blue moon", while thinking "about a cool ending
to a story that ended too soon" on such a smoldering night—
trying to "bring back the feeling" to this plate—what feeling?
The feeling of a bitter-sweet *Blitz* on that bitten tongue...

JEFFREY JOHNSON

Summernight

i reach out across the darkness
part the sheets to touch you
a hand crosses the space between
to find your skin
warm, smooth, soft
hands move up & down
your contours & openings
you come close to touch
my fingers caress, explore
seek sensitive protrusions
move in around & under
your hand clasps me
we sculpt each other
into becoming
into being
touch & reflex
sheets wet & tangled
bind & hold
move with determination
tensions rise & rise & rise
break like the waves
on an empty beach
pound & release & heal
roll, toss, turn
till all dissolves & dissipates
we enter an eternal stillness
for a moment
prolonged
to settle in warm embrace
bundled in white linens
to sleep, to sleep
perhaps to dream

Bathed

in the moonlight
seaside onsen
with the Shinto gods
about our bath
a round moon
reflected & refracted
on the surface
begging to be captured
undulating enticingly
at the slightest movement
wet skin
contours
to explore
rounded
inviting
concave
these waters
shape your movements
the siren
beckons
i
torn
between
the moon
& your call
lost forever
in the split
between celestial
& terrestrial
to neither
do i belong
but to you
Aphrodite

ROBERT MOREAU

Ode Interrupted

I sat down to write
an ode to the
— you snuck up behind me —
beauty of Infinity

My pen glided
like a feather across the
— your arms surrounded me —
frayed edge parchment

Images sang like music as
each lyrical line appeared upon the
— I felt your heat upon my back —
paper emerging in verse

My ode took to the sky through
words carefully chosen in the
— your lips kissed my neck gently —
stellar regions of my mind

My hand reached for
the pen suddenly dropped and the
— your voice whispered yes —
universe stopped in its tracks

Infinity must wait
I am yours

Naked

Illuminated
combinations
subtle vibrations
alabaster translucence
on a silken eiderdown

Soft edged motion
in sudden transformation
passion essence
random excitement
in the slightest touches
all measurements set to
thirty-six point four
degrees...

Perfection
is naked

MARIKO KITAKUBO

Three short poems

1
listening to
water sounds
from the beech bark

miss you
so

2
the hummingbird
also joins
our breakfast

your shining lips

honey

3
forget
your sad days

shining:
his tanned collarbone

age sixteen

KAORI SHOJI

Open and Clamp

This is supposeta hurt, right? I try to ask, or maybe to declare
As the dentist presses his chest against my shoulder to
Contemplate a wisdom tooth
Extraction - any minute now
I will start crying because it's been
Thirty-odd hours since I saw you last and
Knew (oh yeh, I'm not a complete idiot) that it was
Over

Dentist sensei can you please shut up
Just press chest there the warmth of it
Kinda sorta filling a gaping void
in me. uh-huh.
What the fuck why did I
come here today what holy hell was I thinking
Oh yeh the pain I was hoping the pain of this
Extraction
Will somehow override the other thing
Like, priorities or the hierarchies or whatever
You get it, right?
At least I think I do
Ouch

JAKE ADELSTEIN

Cavity

In the chair, she's anxious
As I lean in closer, her pain goes somewhere
Yet her heartache's a challenge
She doesn't say the words
But I can hear her soul:

> Dentist sensei, keep the chatter at bay,
> Press my chest, let its warmth come my way,
> Filling the void that won't fade, won't sway,
> An ache inside me, it's here to stay

She wonders aloud why she's here in my chair
> What was she thinking?
> To trade love's sorrow for a dental affair?
> To override emotions, choose pain?

Can the agony of this filling truly erase
The love that's now lost, in these sterile days?

I get it, in so many ways

Who can forget those summer nights?
Such a beautiful woman
What foolish man could ever despise her?

As I work on her tooth, I can't help but see
She's not the only one with heartache
I too bear a wound, a love long lost
Neither one able to calm our own misery
The teeth heal and no pain remains
But a broken heart…

ELYSIAN

Dear Peter

You drowned yourself
when they removed
your mate
from the tank

I think we've all been there

What if you had waited?

Romeo was wrong—
you could've
been too,
by that logic

Someday maybe
they will accept
dolphin-human
relationships

A lot of unusual relationships
are accepted these days

If you hadn't killed
yourself, and she hadn't
subsequently gone crazy,
maybe you'd have been
eligible for a tax break

Already, it is said
in certain new age circles
that human men and women
are created by materials
from different planets

Why should it be so
mysterious or outlandish
for a young, impressionable,
and intelligent dolphin to
fall in love with
a human woman?

After cohabiting with her
for several months
in captivity,
it seems a little bit
natural

Especially considering
there were also
drugs and
orgasms involved

Who is there really
to judge when
we are dealing
with true love?

BARBARA SUMMERHAWK

Dear Future,

I've always loved you, loving your
Promises hidden between the lines of my face;
Laying down with you in the pastures of my past
Parchment covering our private parts,

We embrace passionately, you
Stroke my longings for a
Future perfect tense.

Hiding out in the Here and Now,
Shoving our cushions aside,
I want some assurance you'll be there for me and
All my fractal worlds.
We can vow at the altar to accept our
Mortal truth but
Our world sometimes seems a run-on sentence
Being shouted from the four corners of the
Earth
Abides, is turning slaphappy inhaling all that carbon,
Coughing
Clearing the Amazons out of the
Tree houses of our angst and ennui
From dusk 'til dawn
Streaks across the west
Is burning
Tie your shoes and get to work with this woman,
Allow all our links to be bug free and fill us all with
Serenity
The logo of my letterhead
Begs that promise
I look forward to meeting you again
I'm back on the bus.
Love, barb

NADIA ARIOLI

Grendel's Mother Considers Eve

im sorry
i was looking
for lilith

MAT CHIAPPE

Polyglot Erotica

Say something, whatever
and we'll invite you to our party
Speak! Comment! Pronounce!
Bring your secret code and disclose it
translate in our ears, say your talky talk
do it declareback, speaker, do it naggy-style
bellow our whistles, roll in the say, do us a crow job
let's do a screechsome, call the way, your phrase or mine?
you are text machine, baby, a text symbol, text us up
let your hoot fetish loose and preach us your hum shot
scream a voicegasm from behind that drawl gag
to make all silencers and mutes know their offense
Punish! Drown! Castigate!
Put them on their knees and make them lick
the cold metallic edges of that semicolon.

Safeword

I crawl down my dungeon
put a choker round my voice
gag my babbling preoccupations
and handcuff all my ambitions
then kill myself
desecrate my metaphors and smiles
crush the last shards of my memories
and persecute the believers of my faith
private desolate eternity
until I wake up with myself
smell my scent and feel my warmth
every inch of my body whispering
that I'll have to be stronger next time
if I truly want to forget.

JOAN ANDERSON

Older Skin

Is like a comfortable suit
With more room for movement
More imagination,
less coyness,
More impatience,
less chances for
The heavenly rough and slow and smooth delights
From a long life's menu full
Of extra juicy toppings.

So while you're in your body suit
Dip into my body fruit
Drink up all my body loot
And let me get a-hold of your wee flute…

So what's your favorite smell?

My friendship with Michiko
Began in earnest when I took
A big breath of
stale Starbucked air and
Answered that my best
whiff was
The rancid curl
Of fresh sweat from
The hot, wet
Armpits of
the man who had just been
Rising,
riding hard for the finish
in and up
on me

TIM EXLEY

Dis-connected

Just words...
But
No measure
of heart twisted...
pain
contained within
words came softly
"We'll meet again"

gaze connected
I froze
absolute zero
no words.
I cried...
that night,
and the day
and then again
days upon days
I wept
uncontrollably...
just yesterday
deep HEAVING
gut wrenching,
intestine twisting
sobs of existential pain
fire and brimstone
my soul melted in the inferno
again
and again
Is this union with the divine?

ALLAN LAKE

At The Galleon

I've ridden to The Galleon on my rusty
old bike that no upwardly-mobile thief
would steal. Here for the fruit toast,
espresso, music and atmosphere.
Pigeon strolls under the old Arborite table
as casual as, but my focus is elsewhere.
If still in the spring of life, I'd propose
to dark, delish, springy-haired waitress.
Course I would. And she'd probably
say, *Yeah, okay* like she was just waiting
for anyone to ask and we'd rent a place
and have a kid named Bozo and mongrel
mutt named King Arfer. Why Not Dept.

The Galleon never disappoints or changes
or disappoints by changing. The 1950s
retired here in this beachside burb of
Melbourne, Oz. Colorful Arborite tables
and worn-out, semi-padded chairs.
Canadian thing, Arborite; my Canadian
parents had such a 'dining' set so I feel
at home, which should aid digestion.
How this rundown place avoided
evolving is a sleepy dog I want to let
lie just out on the dogpissy footpath.

Oblivious potential partner, Galleon Gal,
takes a break, reads Atwood and picks at
scrambled egg. Pigeon, escorted earlier
from crummy old concrete floor, waltzes
back in as if recently returned from abroad,
fully expecting to be feted, shown to its
favorite table. The Galleon is such a place
and becalmed, like so many, I sit idle
on a wee, dark, double sea of caffeine.

TAYLOR MIGNON

Ball Blues

Ego hangs
in my balls
a bag of bruised
grapes she tests me
as she puts down men's
testes: ballego bleedoistic. Soul
slippery as eel b-go only finest of
wines, mine on reserve for you, my partner
WOMAN whose butt bops a hoopla. Surely your
beauty beats the beast of man, unblown away,
yet blown away, i say pop goes the weasel
my fruition brought to a ruin on my purple
easel. Expertly hand-chosen, they do
wish to be plucked up like a ball-
erina off the balls of her feet,
but the edges of her
head-butt strength
cuts the skin
bluntly.

¿Gay is Tay, Tay is Gay?

O! Jean Genet, yr Lady of the Flowers, the argot of the hard lock

gestures' hidden meanings

O! Orchestral Maneuvres in the Dark, you sound camp, yet yr Enola Gay aint

O! Mishima Yukio, you advertised for a wife in the Asahi Evening News

posed as St. Sebastian for the Eiko Hosoe Ordeal by Roses

the martyr turned you on; Confessions of a Mask

Gertrude Stein: A rose is a rose is a rose

O! Magnetic Fields, the Strange Powers

of Stephin Merritt merits flames meritoriously

O! I just can't get enough of the Depeche Mode I Just Can't Get Enough

(In high school didn't know Morrisey was queer, What Difference Does it Make?)

O! If I were a woman I could get unicornily rainbowed Air Rifts

& wouldn't blush to buy yoga pants & clam-digger capris

* * *

Lincoln, Nebraska said to host as many gay men per capita as San Fran

Summertime flashback

walking home along the route past the Children's Zoo

jogger whips out dick in a flash, Ooooooh

High School party at mansion; as acid kicks in

my friend Todd opens the closet & beckons me in, ohhhhhh

never went in nor out

Dry in Cedar Rapids, IA, Cheshire cat, handsome hippy patron of Chicago Fries

invites me to his place to get high

picks up porno & as we watch says go ahead & beat off, O?

My creative writing teacher who made

"Kyoto the center of American poetry in Japan"

hits on me at the bus stop, keeps his orientation a secret

while espousing total poetic transparency

& berating a lesbian poet busted for Chiba Chiba

As Ouroboros, the opposites shift & blends

forever turning in on themselves, within us worlds contained:

the sensitive poet & the goalkeeper jock who loves the spa w/ bath salts

new halves on both sides, women & men redefine themselves, ordinary or nonbinary?

Hello canary fighting hairy fairy; to be adored by both, the audience not contrary.

Hereto hetero, or the devil's 3-way a possible gateway?

S/he'd have to be hotter than hell, licking my taint.

SERGIO A. ORTIZ RIVERA

Photographs

I keep getting ass pics
when what I want to see
are you and me old together
like stale breadcrumbs

I gaze at the man
I'm with, my summer
climb, nothing to stop us
from trailblazing joy

We listen to a song
from Camila, *caliente, caliente*
frío y caliente. Hot, hot, cold & hot.
The beach & the daiquiris
are amazing.

Elusive Minstrel With the Sugarcane Voice

One step forward
and I forget
where, why, what for.
I know that as long
as I reach for a couple
of shooting stars I'll ride
on buttered pancakes
with pixie pears,
milk & honey
all the way to heaven.

Two steps backwards,
grew a belly,
I gained new dreams.
Stopped to observe, absorb,
short term adventures
of mindfulness.
Changes in the decor

of my spacecraft,
my living room.

Time nails me
to the mahogany
of simple new visions.
I went bald. Wrote verses,
songs to calm storms
now forgotten.
Love between two men
a prism, hologram of aging hearts
come to life. My perennial collection
of erotic Dali & Picasso
memories in bed.

Three steps ahead of death,
I am not willing to kneel
to reduce pain. I prefer to return
to secret kisses & sonnets,
men in nostalgic *leather or rubber
outfits* under the shadows in ill-lit
parks on your shores & mine.

NDABA SIBANDA

She Didn't Know

he gave her an unchained look

that had the lady leave her food

untouched and uneaten on a table

it was not a peep or a stolen look

a gaze that unlocked her emotions

she didn't know why she was leaving

Times When Rituals Are Drunk

sometimes in winter a little bolt of heatwave

just springs up and wakes up the dead and dull

at times summer comes with unseasonal chillness

sometimes nightfall is a peep of sunset and light

at times an ant shakes up an elephant into a whimper

there are times when chillness is hotter than any heat

MARCELLUS NEALY

2:15

It's 2:15
I remember the low quake
The humming machine
Telling time to an illusion
Of love left martyred
By this knife

I conjure your face
Whispering "choudai"
To be fed
With the sum of my worth
Hand cranked
Holy water
Weeping from your chin

It's 2:20
I'm almost there
I can hear you
As if you were
Kneeling
At the bedside

"Chodai! Choudai"

Knuckles blurred
Shallowed breathing
Flashback
A winter kiss
The nights we moaned
To cicada songs
And ran round
London streets
In a shopping cart
Rum hazy
Forgetful of the rain

Phantom fingers on my thighs

Faster now
Till I writhe an epileptic twitch
That sends you back
To Hackney
on the last bit of air
I breathe

JOHN FRANCIS CROSS

Holland—Dusseldorf: Hard Border

Hitchhiking out of Holland, three men picked me up near the German border and took me to stay in a Dusseldorf suburb. They were very kind but I showered with a knife by the soap. At night we smoked dope and they urged me to show my bare feet. One wall was papered with a photo of beautiful life-sized trees. When I took off my socks they were so pleased they didn't want me to stop. I was eighteen and looked deceptively creamy. But their seduction went limp, which I've regretted since, for their sake and their generosity, not mine.

Perpignan—Pamplona: Fiesta and Darkness

I hitchhiked from Perpignan to the Pamplona fiesta, sleeping one night in a Barcelona park, another in a rocky field, and arriving at midnight with a Basque nationalist driver who spat when stopped by *Guardia Civil*. Drunks poured wine down my throat from leather skins until two Kiwis offered me room in their riverside tent with two Minnesota women. In the darkness one told of being raped in an alley back home. "Why didn't you fight back?" one guy asked. When I went outside she followed, calling my name. She held me saying, "Fighting back isn't so easy, you know?"

Paris: Beautiful and Unforgotten

In Paris looking for dishwashing work, I dossed in a dirty Pigalle hotel infested with rats. On Sunday I sat outside the Pompidou Centre listening to a rock band sing *I was born in a crossfire hurricane*, ten times. A girl my age spoke to me. We went back to her place with another boy, who disappeared. "My cousin, not my boyfriend," she said. "Let's spend the night together." We kissed and I undressed her. "Slowly," she said. We drank vodka, made love, and she told me her sad story. Her name was a beautiful sound that I've never forgotten.

Tokyo: Popular

After landing in Tokyo, I took two days' training as an English conversation teacher. When a secretary introduced me to colleagues they looked me over open-mouthed. One said, "You don't look English." Another: "Is your hair dyed?" Later the deputy head said, "You look like the kind of person who knows all the words to *Summer Holiday*." (Cliff Richards and the Shadows, 1963.) But the students liked me. One loved me: "I love you," she said, fourteen-years-old and wearing metal teeth braces like a horror villain. They liked my name, too. They all knew somebody with a dog called *John*.

TRACY SHERMAN

Pilgrimage

Your body is a pilgrimage

I begin my trek in the dark jungle of your long black hair
It flows over your shoulders the way the parasitic orchids cover the top of the rainforest

In the shells of your ears I can hear the ringing of the sea waves and taste the salt spray as
I lick their edges

My tongue climbs the dunes of your cheekbones until it finds a moment's rest in the cool
sea of your mouth ringed by the red coral of your lipstick

I transverse your chin into the hollow of your neck where I set up my camp of kisses and
rest until daybreak

My journey starts at sunup as I move to the foothills of your breasts
I surmount them ever so slowly and with great care until I reach the sweet apex

I spend much too long there but it feels like only moments until the sun is down and I
must make camp for the night on the soft sweetness at the top

Down I go the next morning over the wasteland of your belly
My tongue takes a quick rest in the dip of your belly button but I have no time to tarry
long

My kisses make their way over the smooth skin of your hipbone
Mirroring in its way the curve of your cheekbones

As my pilgrimage's goal mirrors the sweet succulence of your lips
I am almost there but there is one more hill covered with a thick and fragrant forest of
hair

My tongue and lips forge through touching and tasting
But I must not exhaust myself as my desire is in sight

My tongue slides down and my pilgrimage is at an end
I have reached the oasis and now the pleasure begins

Inappropriate

So… my girlfriend Setsuko and I are looking for a place to fuck. This is not as easy as it may seem, not in Tokyo with our tiny apartments. And not when one has his 15-year-old son living with him and she is married.

Now in New York City fucking is not so difficult, despite children, husbands, or wives.

You hop in a cab and, if your timing is right and you're agile enough, you both have your underwear off by the time the cab has stopped in front of your friend's Lower East Side tenement.

He's letting you use the place because the landlord just sprayed for the bedbug infestation and you're the Guinea pig. That's right you're the test subject to see if the bedbugs are gone and if the poison from the spray has dissipated.

You check to see if you haven't left your or your girl's "dainties" in the backseat and give the poor cabbie a big tip for putting up with your impromptu strip show.

Then it's a five-flight walk-up, five flights plus landings.

You manage to find his door after the oxygen returns to your lungs. It was five flights plus landings remember?

Open the door and fall face-first onto his king-size waterbed that takes up 3/4 of his apartment. Your girl follows you immediately and it's just as well because as the tidal wave starts you realize you're so exhausted from the taxi cab contortions and the five flights. Plus landings.

You just let the waterbed do all the pushing and thank God you have taken off your underwear in the cab.

Then you hope at least he has something good in the refrigerator to snack on afterward. If there's anything Jewish boys like as much as sex it's having a little nosh post coitus.

Now as titillating as this Showtime soft-core rip-off sounds, it's not something that you can re-create here in Tokyo.

First of all, everybody lives with their parents or some relative or everybody has a husband or wife. So there will be no commandeering anyone's apartment.

Of course, there are love hotels in Japan but Setsuko says only whores go to love hotels for sex.

So she comes up with the bright idea of going to the zoo.

Noted: Regarding sex for Setsuko, the zoo's good, and the love hotel's bad.

Don't get me wrong, I love the zoo. What Bronx boy doesn't, but going to the zoo to have sex? It sounds too much like a Prince song to me.

I am not a prude as you should well know. I mean I like giving and getting everything from anal to zelophilia. But I've never been one for outdoor sex—I mean I like to be comfortable, and I don't want people watching me. In New York, a crowd forms if you unzip your pants for a quick jerk or two.

Anyway, I meet Setsuko at the Ueno Zoo gate and she's carrying something that looks like a giant condom package. What did I get myself into?

"What's that?" I ask.

"It's a tent. It's a little heavy so please carry it."

I already told you that Jews like to snack after schtupping and I'm already schlepping a bag of deli rejects. You've got to make do when you're in Japan.

I take her tent but I'm not happy about the whole idea. Now despite putzing around in the desert for 40 years, Jews are not known for our camping acumen and the idea of putting up a tent let alone fucking in one is not very appealing. But she is very appealing so as can be expected in these situations I go along with the deal.

This is a pretty big zoo, it's no Bronx Zoo but it's pretty big and she finds an out-of-the-way spot under some trees. We sit down to make camp and I spend the rest of the afternoon trying to put up this fercockter tent.

It took me 20 minutes just to unzip the cover and then the thing popped out with an eagerness I could only admire. The thing was like some mad untamed origami.

I spent the next hour and a half wrestling with it but I could never get the damn thing to even vaguely resemble a tent. She's spending most of this time drinking and laughing at me until we both pass out from exhaustion and heat under the tree.

I don't know how long we were there but the next thing I hear are these amazingly loud announcements in half a dozen languages telling us that the zoo is closing and that if we don't get out in 15 minutes the gates will be locked.

I've never been religious so I know I haven't a prayer of getting the tent zippered back up. I folded it as best I could and shoved it with the rest of my things into my bag, half of it hanging out behind my back like a particularly ugly goiter.

It's almost dark by now and we're stumbling our way to where we think the main gate is when suddenly all the zoo lights are turned off.

"This is it," I said, "we're gonna die in a zoo."

"If we're going to die," Setsuko says, "we should at least die with smiles on our faces."

She gives me a look, bends over the railing in front of one of the cages, and hikes up her dress.

I said I'm not one for sex in public but it was almost pitch black, there was no public here, and this may very well have been my last chance.

I sidle up behind her and as we're moaning and groaning we hear a similar sound coming from the cage in front of us.

We can't see a thing but these sounds only serve to further our enthusiasm.

Suddenly we hear stamping in the leaves and a bright light flashes in our direction.

"Everything OK here?" the Zoo Park Ranger asks. We both turn to him sheepishly and he says, "Yeah, it looks like everything's under control."

I turn around and by the light of the flashlight, I see in the cage in front of us a male and female gorilla in the exact same position as we are in.

And I'll be damned if that gorilla didn't wink at me.

ROBOT BASTARD

Causal Response

Mercurial mixture drains from incubation tanks
Sinews sewn together with polymorphic metals awaken

Centuries have passed

They both stand
Staring into the eye
Of a star going supernova

Bionic implants covering their skin twitches

Senses return

A vibration in their skulls
Shocks dormant memories free

Fragments
Of burning civilizations
Shards of light
A cold and wet ground

Cords wrap around their bodies
and insert into the implants
They are connected

Their duty known
To pilot this vessel

Avoid destruction to the last ones
Who slumber below

As they get pulled to the ground
Their nervous system is converted into a navigation device
They observe each other

Through several lifetimes their emotions have eroded away

Yet still an echo beats

He reaches out his hand
But it is pulled back
By his maker's design

Immobile and inert
Their course is now known

Battles are waged within cerebral cortexes
Systems are melted down
Deprogramming and reprogramming sequences are initiated

Their blood takes the worst of it
As it boils for their disobedience
Their systems being brought offline

Not without one last act of rebellion
A push
        That sends the ship sailing into the dying star
                The last of their kind extinguished
                                        In an instant

Jumpstart

1   **INT. LIVING ROOM - NIGHT**

        A brownstone tenement in
        Harlem. Bottle smashes
        against the wall. A
        disheveled shirtless man
        (37) breathes heavily.

                 MASASHI
             It just won't
             come anymore.

        A buxom brunette woman
        (27) dressed head to toe
        in latex slaps him in the
        face.

                 BELLONA
               (authoritative)
             Shut your stupid
             fucking mouth.
             Here, here.

        She thrusts a yellow legal
        pad at him and pushes
        him towards the desk. He
        stumbles and takes a seat.
        Looks at all the half-
        finished notes strewn over
        it. Bellona stomps towards
        him and flings all the

detritus off the table.

                BELLONA
          You need what?
          Inspiration?

                MASASHI
          It's not that, I
          just feel that
          everything I write
          is mediocre, it's
          empty. I'm empty.

                BELLONA
          Ah, you need to
          be filled?

She grabs a bottle of
whiskey and pulls out the
stopper with her teeth.
Yanks his head back by the
hair and pours a generous
serving down his throat.

                MASASHI
             (spluttering)
          What the fuck?!

                BELLONA
          Some music perhaps?

She kicks the sound system
and "Raining Blood" by
Slayer plays.

147

                    BELLONA
                 Now write!

Masashi writes
frantically. Smoke pours
out the end of the pen.
Fire embers jump from the
page and ignite the notes
on the ground. The living
room is now set ablaze.
She pulls out a bullwhip
and starts flogging his
back.

                    BELLONA
                 You feel filled now?

                    MASASHI
                 Yes, my mistress.

FADE TO BLACK

The Plumber Calls

1   **INT: APPARTMENT — DAY**

        A loud knock raps at the door.

                        CINDY
                Who is it?

        The door swings open
        revealing a tall plumber,
        his hammer swinging
        pendulously from his
        toolbelt.

                        JOE
                I'm Joe, you call
                for a plumber?

                        CINDY
                Hey there, I'm
                Cindy and there's
                a problem with my
                pipes.

        He strides purposefully towards
        the kitchen.

2   **INT: KITCHEN — DAY**

        A well-kept kitchen
        containing appliances from
        the 1960s, a sea of teal
        and pastel pinks.

                    JOE
          I can loosen them
          up for ya. They
          just need some...
          lubrication.

He produces a vat of
industrial-strength lube.
Then he proceeds to rip off
the doors under the sink
and lie down on the floor.

                    JOE
          Looks like these
          pipes haven't
          been serviced in
          a long time.

Cindy flutters over to him.

                    CINDY
               (huskily)
          No, they haven't.

He pulls out a big wrench
and starts banging away.

                    JOE
          You might want to
          stand back. You
          could get wet.

Joe opens up the pipe and
dips his fingers into the
vat of lube. Cindy strolls
over to a nearby chair and

pushes her crotch up against it. His
fingers glide effortlessly into the pipe
opening, teasing out whatever is in
there. She gyrates faster against the
chair. Suddenly his whole hand slips
through the pipe.

                    JOE
          I found what's been
          causing the issue.

He pulls out a soggy meatball.

                    JOE (CONT'D)
          You should be more
          careful with these
          balls.

Cindy leans over him, her cleavage
inches from his face.

                    CINDY
          I think I know how to handle
          them.

Joe stands, unbuttons his shirt, and
puts his hand on her hip.

                    JOE
          Well we should probably
          settle up.

                    CINDY
              (exasperated)
          Yes, we should.

                    JOE
          That'll be seven dollars and
          sixty-nine cents.

She drops her teddy revealing lacy pink
lingerie.

                    CINDY
                   (coyly)
          Is there any other way I could
          repay you?

Joe picks up the vat of lube and grins.
He goes into his pants and unfurls a
long, thick receipt.

                    JOE
          So that will be seven
          ninety-five including tax.

She pulls out a crisp ten-dollar bill
from her bra and hands it to him.

MIRACLE JONES

An excerpt from "Sex Reviews"

The apartment of young Jack and Quinn is sparse but for a few sticks of anorexic furniture—catalog stuff which is simultaneously overdesigned and uninviting, ectopic roods as thin and cheap as complimentary pens from a bank. The palette is salmon and seawater. Hardwood here instead of carpet.

There are toys everywhere—children's toys, I mean—round, colorful plastic ersatz fruit, facsimile pots, counterfeit meats, and simulated cheeses. There are low gates at either end of the living room, which I presume are intended to kettle a small child. In this matryoshka of penitention, the fenced-in living room also contains an empty playpen. This Playskool panopticon even has an exercise yard: from my seat on the punishingly-hard couch I can see that there is a bungee cord that swings up to the lintel of the kitchen door and which is attached to tiny mechanical legs. The rotors and servos for this kiddie-mech—surely an infernal machine meant to exhaust springy toddler quads!—are currently powered down.

The room is lit by candlelight, which feels like a rare thrill for this infant-forward space. Single candles also light the bathroom, the kitchen, and the back bedroom.

Quinn sits between me and Jack on the couch. She is touching him and not touching me. Quinn is wearing giant hoop earrings and little else. She seems self-conscious in her crisp bra and black panties. She keeps scratching her upper arm, like a junky coming down. Perhaps the cold winter evening is causing her to have an outbreak of dry skin? Jack's nerves are also as frayed as split-ends: he could churn butter with his joggling knees.

Jack and Quinn are both quite attractive, especially for young parents who almost certainly aren't getting enough sleep. Like many college-crucible couples, they look alike: they both have upturned button noses and a jangly enthusiasm that would be engaging if it weren't poisoned by too much time spent as cellmates. The grim, isolating cult of parenthood has made them punch-drunk and viperous. On some unspoken level, they hate each other very deeply. I'm already making predictions for their humping: first they will show off, and then will travel down a well-worn groove.

"It's rare around here that no one is shitting themselves and asking me to deal with it," says Quinn. She looks at me expectantly, but I don't respond. She keeps trying to look at my notes, which is why I'm not taking very many.

"We can be as loud as we want tonight," says Jack.

I drink the dregs of my cup of coffee, and then move to a hard-backed chair across the room. Jack seems to relax when I am no longer seated next to his trouble and strife.

"Should I start?" asks Jack, looking at me. Quinn bites his earlobe in an overdetermined gesture of performative lust that curdles my guts. I would rather watch them bicker about unwashed dishes than reenact dick-less cable softcore.

"We're supposed to act like we're alone," says Quinn. Yes, please do act like you are alone.

Quinn gets down off the couch, flicking her hair at me. I quail at this essential dishonesty, but remain externally placid so as not to throw too many rocks into their evaporating sex pond. She leans down without bending her knees, flexing her legs and ass. She turns around and pushes her spread cheeks into her husband's face, swirling her anus around his mouth and nose like she is smearing his dopy face with a piece of wedding cake. He rubs her thighs and pushes her down so that she straddles his crotch. She sits on him for a moment, and then she swings over to kiss him. He bends back awkwardly against the couch cushions.

In her black lingerie, Quinn is a perfect avatar of catalog model sexuality. She is shabby voluptuous. Her panties are see-through enough that I can tell she has recently shaved and applied some concealer. Jack keeps looking at me and giving me an embarrassed grin. Look what he has stolen from the universe! Look what he has won with his stupendous male exertions! And yet, his essential hate of his wife remains.

Quinn squats between Jack's legs. She unzips his pants and breathes on his crotch through his underwear, like his genitals are spectacles that she's about to wipe clean with a dampened cloth.

She pushes her breasts together and rubs them against Jack's knees and then swings her hair into his face. Her swinging hair comes perilously close to one of the candles. Suddenly, the distance between her hair and the open flame is all I can think about. I try to blow the candle out from where I am sitting without interrupting them, but my clandestine exhalations only make the flame shudder. I try to create a draft with my notepad, but this is even less effective.

Quinn lifts Jack up to help him get his pants down around his ankles. I bend forward, intrigued. She does this with the same economy of movement that she must harness when she changes a diaper. For a moment there is the palpable feeling of true tenderness between them. He is trapped there on the couch with his pants shackling him. Exposed, we see that he is still completely soft. His testicles are hairless, waxed, and lovingly powdered. His penis dangles, flaccid and non-threatening, like a twisted aglet from a pair of comfortable old sweatpants.

I cross my legs. His softness is a challenge. An invitation to drama. I make a few quick sketches. I'm practiced enough by now that my eyes do not leave his inert vascular nugget.

"I'm sorry," he says. On my pad, I write the word "contrition" and underline it hard.

"It's been a long week," says Quinn.

 Quinn looks back at me. I put my pen down and steeple my fingers. I try not to even breathe loudly. This is a hostile softness; a softness that provokes.

"You like this?" she asks him. She tries to stimulate him in basic genre fashion. She gets aggressive, squeezing his balls and sticking one nail-polish-free finger shallowly into his rectum, but this does nothing. She stands up and leads him into the bedroom. I follow at a respectful distance.

"I'm going to fuck your whole stupid face," she says. "Lay down, bitch. Stiff upper lip!"

With deliberate, theatrical assertiveness, Quinn pushes her husband down onto his back. He yelps, popping back up immediately. He removes several giant-sized pink toddler Lego from beneath him, tossing them across the room with real irritation.

The abundance of toys makes me hope briefly that one of these primary-colored measles will end up inside somebody's asshole or clamped down between someone's quivering jaws. Jack stands up.

"Help me," he says.

He and Quinn shake the comforter clean of stuffed ponies, plastic donuts, and pacifiers. Will any of these toys be repurposed for erotic exploration? Such banal, scenery-chewing deviance is all I can hope for at this point.

Quinn pushes Jack back down again on the bed and squats over him.

Finally, we establish a propulsive narrative arc! Quinn grinds her haunches on her husband's face, mashing her (shorn, reddened) clunge into his mouth and chin, obscuring him completely. She erases her husband with her angry pussy, stropping her pissjaws on his stubble and nose cartilage like she is a dog wiping herself on newly cut grass.

A good critic reviews what is put before them. A good critic does not attempt to improve on what an artist presents. A good critic does not offer alternatives and instead wrangles with the subject matter and themes that are presented. I accept that this will be The Sex.

What does this cruel, frustrated pussy levigation mean? It is clear that Quinn's mastery of her husband's face as a sexual device is total. A thin trickle of plasmic fluid runs down his neck. She puts her hands over her head and joins them together, like a boxing champ after a knockout. This gives her more torque and greater balance to more effectively sandpaper his wriggling mouth.

Jack makes fists as Quinn fucks his face. For a moment, Quinn and I both find ourselves staring at his soft cock. We catch each other staring. We lock eyes and then we each look away. She grinds harder, leaning down to squeeze his balls experimentally as he pounds the bed with his newly formed fists. She runs her asshole all the way from his forehead to his chin, letting him lick the entire length of her, and then she resumes her scrubbing.

Is sexual chemistry just a mild allergy that we have to each other? Is it only when chemistry finally wears off that we can begin to effectively use each other like the objects that we actually are?

"I'm going to come," she says absent-mindedly. Jack hits the bed over and over again like a pro-wrestler hamming it up as she shudders into his face, urinating a little down his chin.

"mmmmffffffcococllll," he says from beneath her.

"mmmgdoosssssslllll?" he asks.

She doesn't get up. Two stars.

Bios

Jake Adelstein is an American journalist, crime writer, and blogger based in Japan. He is the author of *Tokyo Vice: An American Reporter on the Police Beat in Japan*, which in 2022 was made into an HBO Max television series of the same name. IG: @tokyovice

Vincent Aimée, based in Japan, is a photographer and visual artist celebrated for a sensual and erotic aesthetic. Their distinctive style crafts captivating visual narratives, immersing audiences in thematic explorations through science-fiction, futurism, surrealism, and eroticism. Embodying a broad spectrum of interests from fashion to fetishes, Vincent's work serves as a profound medium for communication and self-expression. Through art, Vincent establishes a unique dialogue with the audience, marking a distinctive footprint in the contemporary art sphere.

Self-taught, **Farah Ali** lives by the sea in the UK, where she channels her melancholy and love of nature into fiction and poetry. She has a particular affinity for the short form. Award-nominated and featured in several anthologies, she has been published and has upcoming publications in a variety of reputable online and print journals including *contemporary haibun online*, *Bones*, *chrysanthemum*, *Macqueen's Quinterly*, *Akitsu Quarterly*, *right hand pointing*, *petrichor*, *tiny wren lit*, *Acorn*, *Modern Haiku*, *whiptail*, and *hedgerow*. Her supernatural *Deerleap Hollow Series* is available from Amazon. IG: @farahauthor

Joan Anderson was born in Edinburgh, Scotland and lived in Cambodia before coming to Japan to chase commas and drunk poets. She works as an editor and likes Buddhism, peace, and humans a lot.

Nadia Arioli is the founder and editor-in-chief of *Thimble Literary Magazine*. A three-time Best of the Net and Pushcart Nominee, Arioli's poetry, artwork, and essays can be found in *Rust + Moth*, *Pithead Chapel Hunger Mountain*, *Mom Egg Review*, *Permafrost*, and elsewhere. Arioli's latest collections are with Dancing Girl and Kelsay Books.

Sayaka Asaba (浅葉爽香) is a chimera clad in poetry.

Herman Bartelen spent formative years in London, Ontario in a world of sound poems, performance art, and experimental plays. After moving to Tokyo, he became more involved with lyric and play writing, as well as photographic and visual art. In the last two years, he has turned his keyboard back to more poetry.

Made from found parts on a distant planet, **Robot Bastard** has spent most of his existence endeavoring to understand water-based organisms. His central processing unit has often gone into disrepair and now resides in Japan, in order to get regular maintenance and report his findings.

Sanjay Bradford is a street photographer who roams the streets. When he sees a scene he can't take his eyes off of, he knows right then and there that he has got to get a picture—has got to press the shutter button at this very spot when the right opportunity comes along.

Philippe Bürgin is a researcher, translator, and poet from the far south of Germany. He received a B.A. in Philosophy and English

Studies from the University of Heidelberg in 2018 and an M.A. in Philosophy of Culture and Art Critique from the Universities of Stuttgart and Paris 8 in 2021. He is currently doing research for a Ph.D. thesis on the aesthetics of the sublime. His associated research on Japanese Aesthetics regularly brings him back to Tokyo, Japan, where he likes to be a guest at Drunk Poets See God.

Kevin Carter is a writer, musician, and technologist whose work has been featured in *MAKE, 2600 Magazine*, and *The Fiction Circus*, among others. He runs the hypermedia reading series Derangement of the Senses and lives and plays laser harp in New York City. You can find more at https://shotintoeternity.com.

Srinjay Chakravarti is a writer, editor, and translator based in Salt Lake City, Calcutta, India. He was educated at St. Xavier's College, Calcutta, and at universities based in Calcutta and New Delhi. University degrees: B.Sc. (Economics honors) and M.A. (English). As a former journalist with *The Financial Times Group*, he has worked on the editorial staff of an international online financial news service. His creative writing, including poetry, short fiction, and translations, has appeared in more than 150 publications in over 40 countries. His first book of poems, *Occam's Razor* (Writers Workshop, Calcutta: 1994) received the Salt Literary Award in 1995 from John Kinsella, the eminent Australian writer and academic. He won one of the top prizes ($7,500) in the Dorothy Sargent Rosenberg Memorial Poetry Competition 2007–08. Please visit his literary website, www.srinjaychakravarti. com., for further details.

Neil Craig Chapman is a Kamakura-based perfume writer at theblacknarcissus.com, a Jasmine Award (fragrance journalism) winner, and author of the book *Perfume: In Search of Your Signature Scent* (2019). He occasionally performs as the drag entity, Burning Bush.

David Chenery is an artist and musician from Victoria, BC, Canada. He currently performs in The Hex, a Death Rock 3-piece, as well with Creep-Rockers Thepurrverts.

Mat Chiappe (b. 1984) is a professor of Japanese Literature at El Colegio de México and a translator of Japanese literature into Spanish and English. He lived seven years in Tokyo during which he did his Ph.D. and taught at Waseda University. Living in Japan nearly destroyed his soul, if it hadn't been for the amazing people he met there and who carry out incredible projects such as ToPoJo. Recently, he has been considering raising his first cat.

Australian born, **Sorcha Chisholm** has been dabbling in poetry since adolescence. To this day she continues to scribble out songs and poems whenever the Muse strikes her with inspiration. This is her second contribution to ToPoJo. In 2013, she and Samm Bennett started up the monthly poetry event Drunk Poets See God. She is currently performing around Tokyo with the murder ballads band The Raven's Tale.

John Francis Cross (1961–2022) was a Tokyo-based poet, performance artist, and experimental filmmaker originally from the UK. He authored five books (*Ghosh in China, Drunk God Sees Poet, I Am Xeluco, 88,* and *100 100-Word True Travel Stories*). In a career spanning the globe, he was Poet-in-Residence at Himalayan Orchard, India, and worked in a variety of countries as a dishwasher, factory hand, farm laborer, reporter, poet, secretary, and teacher of English, China Studies, and Chinese-English Translation.

Datiko was born in SF in '65... Papi from the country of Georgia, Mami from Bogota, Columbia. He was schooled by the Russian Orthodox in the foggy Richmond district. He played classical violin as an adolescent, went Rock in the 70s, traveled extensively in South America & Western Europe. He has lived in SF, Reno, Bogota, Heidelberg, Berkley, Neuchâtel, Paris, Madrid, St. Petersburg, Tbilisi, Salzburg, Barcelona, Torino & Tokyo. He is beloved and blessed by babies.

May Drew is a Tokyo-based artist. She aims to empower women with her digital graphics and hemp yarn art. Her art career started in 2020, and she took a standstill during the COVID-19 pandemic to draw inspiration from Japan's social and cultural issues. Her pieces often capture women's strong and graceful energy.

Sasha Drozd is a Tokyo-based fine art photographer specializing in musicians and performance artists, with a profound fascination for Butoh, underground subcultures, and the multifaceted world of art in all its diversity.

Ryan Dzelzkalns has poems appearing with *Catapult, DIAGRAM, The Offing, The Shanghai Literary Review, Tin House,* and others. He received an M.F.A. from New York University and was awarded the Wendy Parrish Poetry Prize. His writing has been translated into Latvian (the language of his grandparents) and has been anthologized in a handful of collections. He was a recent Fulbright scholar in Tokyo, where he still lives. Read more at RyanDz.com.

Alicia Elkort's first book of poetry, *A Map of Every Undoing,* was published in 2022 by Stillhouse Press with George Mason University, after winning their book contest. Alicia's poetry has been nominated several times for the Pushcart, Best of the Net, and the Orison Anthology, and her work appears in numerous journals and anthologies. She reads for *Tinderbox Poetry Journal* and works as a Life Coach in Santa Fe, NM, where praise and clouds are part of her everyday experience. For more info or to watch her two video poems, visit http://aliciaelkort. mystrikingly.com/.

Michael Ely is a game designer bouncing between Tokyo and California. His poem "Jazz Bar" is shorter than this bio!

Originally from the Great Lakes region of the United States, **Elysian**'s journeys have taken her to many places in Asia. She has lived in and performed poetry in Vietnam, Thailand, and Japan. She is very interested in philosophical and esoteric topics, and her writing is strongly influenced by the principles of Hermeticism. She is also an avid collector of interesting minerals and stones and has her own jewelry brand called Elysium Accessories. IG: @satyrnelysian

The gift of poetry touched **Tim Exley** only recently. Twelve years before life's lottery awarded him a breakdown, transformed, he was thrown fully into the river of existence. Now and then the divine touches him and gifts him with some words. He currently floats between his Chiba-ken abode, the Himalaya, and a few other countries. He welcomes others to join him in travel and exploration of both the inner and outer worlds.

Rachel Ferguson is a Scottish poet, communication coach, and DEI consultant. She posts new work regularly on Instagram @tokyorf. Her debut collection, *Thoughts on Waking*, is available on Amazon. She lives in Tokyo, and in her spare time enjoys singing, and walking in the woods with her children.

Italian/German writer **Alexandra Fössinger** is the author of the poetry collection *Contrapasso* (Cephalopress, 2022). Her multilingual work is published or forthcoming in numerous journals including *Tears in the Fence, Frogmore Papers, Wild Court, High Window, The Journal, morphrog, The Crank, Green Ink Poetry, Oyster River Pages, The Gentian Journal, Reliquiae, La Piccioletta Barca, The Wild Word, Eunoia Review, bind, Die leere Mitte, Mono, Feral,* the *White Stag Publishing's Spirit* anthology, the *Linen Press' Tabula Rasa* anthology, *Full House Literature Magazine,* and *Gyroscope Review.* She is mostly interested in the spaces between things, the tiny shifts in time and space, the overlooked, the unsaid.

Jeremy Gadd is an Australian author and poet whose most recent publication was *Driving Into the Dark,* a selection of 60 previously published poems (Ginninderra Press, Adelaide, 2022). He has M.A. and Ph.D. degrees from the University of New England and lives and writes in an old Federation-era house overlooking Botany Bay, the birthplace of Modern Australia.

Andrew Gebert is a Tokyo-based translator, researcher, and gentleman farmer.

Dr. **Davord Griffiths** is a New Zealand-educated jurist who now plies his trade as an adjunct lecturer across multiple Tokyo university campuses, specializing in constitutional and human rights law. Dr. Griffiths was a co-founder of the Illiterati Theatre Company (now defunct) and played Rosencrantz in the Company's sole production: Tom Stoppard's *Rosencrantz and Guildenstern are Dead* (1966). Griffiths' verse is fashioned after the style of Nicholas Urfe, the failed poet and protagonist of John Fowles' novel *The Magus* (1965).

Robert Holbrook is a self-taught artist who has held exhibitions in Osaka, Seoul, and Tokyo. A global nomad who was born in the United States, he has lived in ten countries and visited another 35. Although a jack-of-all-trades, he makes his living teaching languages, and is an avid armchair linguist. Another hobby of his which borders on being a job is DJing Brazilian and Latin music. He currently resides in Fujisawa.

Bill Howell was born in Liverpool, England, and grew up in Halifax, Nova Scotia. He has lived in Toronto, Ontario, for more than half his life and was a network producer-director at CBC Radio Drama for three decades. With five collections to his credit, his work appears regularly in journals and anthologies across Canada, the UK, Australia, Sweden, and the US. https:///bit.ly/242HowellP

Jeffrey Johnson was a pool-shooting street urchin, a brakeman, and a fruit harvester in other lives. In this one he is a permanent wanderer, who has worked on compiling a Hopi dictionary and has typed several books that include works of literary criticism, poetry, and translations from Japanese. He has also served this journal since its inception and hopes to keep it alive.

Miracle Jones is from Texas. He is a very private person. The story "Sex Reviews" is from the porn collection *Christmas,* which can be read in its entirety at http://miraclejones.com/christmas.html.

Tim Kahl [http://www.timkahl.com] [https://soundcloud.com/tnklbnny] is the author of five books of poems, most recently *Omnishambles* (Bald Trickster, 2019) and *California Sijo* (Bald Trickster, 2022). He is also an editor of *Clade Song* [http://www.cladesong.com]. He builds flutes, plays them, and plays guitars, ukuleles, charangos and cavaquinhos as well. He currently teaches at California State University, Sacramento, where he sings lieder while walking on campus between classes.

Zoria Petkoska Kalajdjieva (Zoria P.K.) is a neo-Tokyoite telling stories about the city in many forms, mostly via cyber[punk] poetry. She also specializes in visual poetry (completed a postgrad research fellowship for Japanese visual poetry at the Tokyo University of Foreign Studies) and is the author of *Zborigami* (*Wordigami*), a book of calligrammes. She is an associate editor at *Tokyo Poetry Journal*, commissioning editor at *Tokyo Weekender* magazine, and editor-in-chief of the poetry journal *III* (published in Macedonia, on hiatus). Zoria devised the Poetry Archeology creative writing method. She still hasn't devised a time machine though.

Jes Kalled is a multidisciplinary artist presently based in Tokyo, Japan. Born and raised in New Hampshire, she studied Film in Prague, Czech Republic at FAMU, and relocated to Japan to pursue art and language after graduating from Smith College with a B.A. in Film Studies and Dance. She works across the mediums of writing, photography, painting, dance, and film, and her work has been published in *Metropolis Magazine* and *Tokyo Weekender*, among others. In June 2023, she held a solo exhibition titled *A year of forgetting the pines* at Gallery Paradiso, investigating the loss of meaning in a relationship, the loss of Arabic language in her family, and a reorientation towards body and un-fragmenting "self." She is also the writer and creator of *Swallow*, a documentation project that plays with memory and location

Mariko Kitakubo (b. 1959) is a Tokyo-based tanka poet, performer, and co-founder of Tan-Ku. She has published seven books of tanka including four bilingual ones—*On This Same Star*, *Cicada Forest*, *INDIGO*, and *DISTANCE*—the last of which was published with Deborah P. Kolodji as the first Tan-Ku collection book. Mariko has also produced a CD of her tanka titled *Messages*, and has performed her poetry on at least 246 occasions and in 56 cities across the world. She hopes to encourage more poetry lovers worldwide to appreciate and practice tanka. https://www.en.kitakubo.com

Allan Lake, originally from Saskatoon, Canada, has lived in Vancouver, Cape Breton Island, Ibiza, Tasmania, Western Australia, and Melbourne. Lake has won Lost Tower Publications (UK) Comp, Melbourne Spoken Word Poetry Festival, and publication in New Philosopher. His latest poetry chapbook (Ginninderra Press) is My Photos of Sicily. Such journals as The Hong Kong Review, Island Magazine, Cordite Poetry Review, StylusLit, Meniscus, Quadrant, American Writers Review, and The Antigonish Review have accepted his work for publication.

Peter Leghorn (B.A. Honors Fine Art) is a native Scottish artist residing in Tokyo, Japan. He mainly works in the fields of drawing and painting. Not bound to any fixed motif, inspiration is drawn from far and wide, creating artwork that challenges perceptions of reality and identity. An array of processes, techniques, or, as the artist sees them, "codes", are woven and layered to create multifaceted imagery that plays with viewers' expectations.

Edward Levinson is a photographer, essayist, and poet living in Japan since 1979. His book *Whisper of the Land* (Fine Line Press, 2014) is a collection of essays based on his life in Japan and includes many bilingual haiku. *Timescapes Japan* (Nippon Camera, 2006), his award-winning photo book, takes one on a black and white pinhole photo journey through Japan. He resides in a countryside paradise on the Boso Peninsula in Chiba Prefecture, where he attunes to nature and the world around him for creative inspiration. Please visit http://www.edophoto.com and http://www.whisperoftheland.com.

Alison Lubar teaches high school English by day and yoga by night. They are a queer, nonbinary, mixed-race femme whose life work (aside from wordsmithing) has evolved into bringing mindfulness practices, and sometimes even poetry, to young people. Their work has been nominated for both the Pushcart & Best of the Net, and they're the author four chapbooks: *Philosophers Know Nothing About Love* (Thirty West Publishing House, 2022), *queer feast* (Bottlecap Press, 2022), *sweet euphemism* (CLASH!, 2023), and *It Skips a Generation* (Stanchion, 2023). You can find out more at http://www.alisonlubar.com/ or on Twitter @ theoriginalison.

PD Lyons was born and raised in the USA and since 1998 has resided in Ireland. Spent a few years before in Cape Brenton, Nova Scotia, where winters are great for writing.

Travelled a bit, worked a lot, raised two wonderful children as well as horses (Morgans, Andalusian Thoroughbred, Irish sport horse etc.) in USA and Ireland. Has worked as dishwasher, floor washer, textile mill laborer, construction worker, pesticide sprayer, fire safety inspector, toy shop manager, substance abuse counselor, women's shoe shop manager, etc. Currently cutting grass in a small medieval village in County Westmeath, Ireland.

Debs Max is often late, occasionally paint-stained.

John Meyer (*The Spilt Ink*) was born in Michigan on a cold October night in 1977. He has exhibited his artwork and/or painted live in the USA, Germany, France, the Netherlands, Greece, and Japan. Currently, you can find him working on commissioned art projects in his studio, exhibiting his artwork at galleries, painting live at music events, or sketching away at cafes in Tokyo.

Taylor Mignon is cofounder of the *Tokyo Poetry Journal*, editing the *Japan and The Beats* book-length edition (v5) and the *Butoh and Poetry* issue (v6). He translated surrealist poet Torii Shōzō (1932–1994) for the collected volume *Bearded Cones & Pleasure Blades* (highmoonoon, 2013). He recently published *VOU Visual Poetry Tokio, 1958–1978* (Isobar Press, 2022) & upcoming is the volume *Neo-Visual Poetry of Japan* (Gaijinsha, 2023).

Yuuri Miki (三木悠莉) is a poetry slammer, slam organizer, poet. Began doing poetry performances around Tokyo in 2012, going on to earn back-to-back national titles as champion of Poetry Slam Japan in 2017 and 2018, representing Japan in the World Cup of Poetry in Paris (the first woman poet to earn the award, and the first person to win twice). In 2017 and 2018, she organized the Ueno Poetrican Jam, Japan's largest ever poetry reading event, drawing over 1900 attendees and bringing in significant NGO and corporate support. From 2020, she co-founded and became the director of KOTOBA Slam Japan. In 2023, she made performance tours in 16 countries in Europe, Central America, and South America, organized by the national poetry slam champions of each country.

Noriko Mizuta (水田宗子) is a poet, translator, comparative literature scholar, former professor at the University of Southern California, former president of Josai International University, former chancellor of the Josai University system, and current chancellor and director of the International Institute for Media and Women's Studies. A pioneer in the translation of works by modern Japanese women writers, beginning with the anthology *Japanese Women Writers: Twentieth Century Short Fiction* (1991). She also helped the field of feminist literary criticism in Japan both through her critical works and through establishing Japan's first doctoral programs in women's studies and gender studies. In English, her poetry has been published in two volumes translated by Jordan A. Y. Smith, *The Road Home* (2015) and *Sea of Blue Algae* (2016).

Robert Moreau is from Canada and is now living in Tokyo. He graduated from York University in Toronto with a B.F.A., and has a Master's Degree in TESOL from Teachers College Columbia University. He is currently an Assistant Professor at Meiji University, where he teaches at the School of Business Administration. Moreau is also an active musician in the Tokyo music scene, specializing in the mandolin. After years of artistic endeavors in the visual and musical arts, he decided during the COVID-19 pandemic to try his hand at poetry. Moreau has performed at open mic events including performances at Drunk Poets See God, a poetry event held in Tokyo.

Jacob R. Moses (AKA Jack M. Freedman) is a poet and spoken word artist from Staten Island, NY. Publications featuring his work span the globe. Countries in which poems found homes include the USA, the UK, Canada, Ireland, France, the Netherlands, Ukraine, Iraq, Nigeria, South Africa, Mauritius, Pakistan, India, Bangladesh, Singapore, and Thailand. He is the author of the full-length poetry book *Grimoire* (iiPublishing, 2021). Currently, he is a graduate student at Southern New Hampshire University pursuing an M.A. in English and Creative Writing.

Marcellus Nealy is a poet, lyricist, photographer, NHK announcer, and associate professor of English and Interpersonal Communication for Health Care at Juntendo University. He is also a lyricist, rapper, and MC for the multi-platinum Japanese pop band Dreams Come True. In 2022, he and Biankah Bailey edited an anthology of poetry and art titled *UMOJA, The Black Diaspora Edition* (Tokyo Poetry Journal). Originally from Cleveland Ohio, he has been living in Japan since 1992. During most of that time, Marcellus has been actively involved in Tokyo's literary and creative arts scenes.

Al Ningen is the winner of the White Enso Spring/Summer 2023 Poetry Prize.

Nishalya is a Sri Lankan writer in her early twenties, at the threshold of her writing career. In the past few years, she's been based in Colombo, Sri Lanka, Kawagoe, Japan, and Fort Wayne, Indiana. She approaches poetry as a tool for expression, contemplation, storytelling, and most prominently, healing. It is a comforting passion of hers that she seeks to grow within. While she finds great pleasure in writing poetry, one of her favorite elements is performing her works. She is grateful to poetry for the space it forces people to claim, and the voice it gives without supposition.

Mihiro Ogawa was born in Kawasaki, Japan, in 1995, and currently lives in Yokohama. He majored in English when he studied at university and graduate school and read a hell of a lot of English books to build his own unique world inside his brain. When he first listened to David Bowie's *Ziggy Stardust* at the age of 17, he decided to be a rock 'n' roller, at least in his mind. He has been an English teacher for about three years, working alternately as either a substitute or a part-time teacher. His favorite things are listening to music, singing songs, playing guitar, writing poems and essays, reading books, newspapers, and dictionaries, walking his dog, and doing kickboxing. He has been too nerdy in his life but is now opening up his mind to people around him to savor his life as much as he can.

Repatriare Perdita is a Canadian who spent most of her adult life in Japan. She is grateful to receive her first publication from ToPoJo and is indebted to the hosts and poets of Tokyo's Drunk Poets See God for the Friday nights of delicious instigation, inspiration, and provocation. You can find more of her work on Instagram @repatriareperdita. These poems are dedicated to JFC and 旦那様.

Jonathan Pessant is a Maine poet and Army veteran. He holds a Master's degree in poetry from the Stonecoast MFA program. His works appear, or are forthcoming, in *Space and Time Magazine*, *Pedestal Magazine*, *Slipstream Press*, and others.

Sarah Sands Phillips (b.Tsí Tkaròn:to, Canada) is a Red River Métis/British artist and poet. Her practice spans painting, photography, moving image, sculpture, and text. She completed an MFA at the Ruskin School of Art at the University of Oxford (2019). She is currently based in Tokyo, Japan.

Ulyses Razo's poems have appeared in or are forthcoming from *Spectra*, *Propel*, *Pity Milk Press*, *Ghost City Review*, *dream boy book club*, *dirt child*, *petrichor*, and elsewhere. He was a 2023 fellow at Paul Smith's College and lives in London. IG: @ulysesrazo

Sergio A. Ortiz Rivera is a retired Educator, Bilingual-Gay PRican Poet, Human Rights Advocate. Pushcart nominee, Best of the Web, Best of the Net. He took 2nd place in the 2016 Ramón Ataz annual poetry competition, sponsored by Alaire Publishing House.

Paul Rowland is originally from the United Kingdom, but he has lived in Japan for 15 years. He has been writing poems and stories for as long as he can remember. He tends to think in terms of books or collections and series, rather than individual poems, because he wants to explore an idea or theme from as many angles as possible. He likes collaborating with artists to combine text with other media, such as paintings, photographs, music, dance, and ikebana. He also enjoys wandering around Tokyo taking abstract photos of urban decay. He tries to pay attention to what is ignored and transform the mundane into something beautiful. He works as an English Literature teacher at an international school in Tokyo.

Simon Scott originates from Christchurch, New Zealand and is a Kamakura-based freelance journalist, editor, teacher, and poet who has been published in a very diverse range of international newspapers, magazines, and literary journals. He is currently working on a master's thesis through the University of Auckland about the Beat Generation, East Asia, and Buddhism.

Tracy Sherman was born in New York City, where he spent his time reading and learning to be a magician. He was a professional performance artist, actor, fire eater, and magician for over 20 years in NYC before permanently moving to Japan, where he teaches English and writes plays, fiction, and poetry. Tracy reads and performs his writing whenever there is an opportunity and an empty stage.

Kaori Shoji is a journalist, writer, and film critic based in Tokyo, Japan who grew up in New York City. She writes in both English and Japanese and has been published in *The New York Times*, *The Washington Post*, *The Japan Times*, *IGN Japan*, *Monocle*, and more.

Ndaba Sibanda is a Bulawayo-born poet, novelist, thought leader, and nonfiction writer who has authored 29 books of various genres and persuasions and coauthored more than 100 books and several peer-reviewed articles. Sibanda's book *Notes, Themes, Things And Other Things: Confronting Controversies, Contradictions And Indoctrinations* was considered for the *2019 Restless Book Prize for New Immigrant Writing in Nonfiction*. His book *Cabinet Meetings: Of Big And Small Preys* was considered for *The Graywolf Press Africa Prize 2018*. Sibanda is a three-time Pushcart nominee.

C. E. J. (Christopher) Simons is Senior Associate Professor of Literature at ICU in Tokyo. His poems and criticism have appeared in publications including *Tokyo Poetry Journal, Times Literary Supplement, The Independent, P N Review, Oxford Poetry, Magma, The Liberal, The May Anthology, Isis,* and *World Haiku.* He has published two poetry chapbooks and three full-length collections with Isobar Press, most recently *Flight Risk* (2021). Major poetry awards include second place in the 2009 Cardiff International Poetry Competition, several prizes in the Wigtown competition, and being twice listed for Canada's CBC Literary Prize (2009 and 2010). In 2003, he held the Harper-Wood Studentship in Creative Writing from St. John's College, Cambridge. He is a former Editor of the Poetry Book Society, London, where he edited their quarterly magazine, the *Bulletin.*

Jordan A. Y. Smith is a producer, writer, researcher, and translator living between Tokyo and Los Angeles. Co-founder of the poetry-technology collective Cōem, producing the 3D audio hologram project GeoPossession (2022). Author of poetry and art volume *Syzygy* (Awai Books, 2020), and co-author of *Sea of Trees* and *√IC: Redux.* Co-founder of KOTOBA, the national poetry slam of Japan. Producer for 23 hours of Naro.tv masterclasses with anime director Oshii Mamoru, Olympic Coach Hayakawa Daisuke, ULTRAMAN director Yagi Takeshi, as well as four BBC Radio programs on Japanese poetry and culture. Translator of many of Japan's leading poets. Curator for DIESEL Art Gallery (Shibuya). After completing a Ph.D. in Comparative

Literature at UCLA, he served as Associate Professor at Josai International University, and taught comparative literature, Japanese studies, and translation at UCLA, Waseda, Sophia, and CSU Long Beach. IG: @jordangiraffe

Greg Snazz was born in Greg Snazz, but currently lives in Greg Snazz. His poems have appeared in Greg Snazz, Greg Snazz, and Greg Snazz. He received an M.F.A. in Greg Snazz in 1977. He is married to Greg Snazz and has two Greg Snazzes.

John Solt is a poet, postcard collagist, and translator. His latest book, *Poems for the Unborn*, is a compilation of 30 years of his poems in GUI (Tokyo), translated by Aoki Eiko, and published by Shichōsha in 2020. Bookmaker Ohie Toshio in 2023 made a special edition of ten copies, and it was displayed at Ohie's retrospective exhibition at the Wakayama Prefectural Museum of Modern Art.

Samuel Louis Spencer is an American journalist and poet. He loves words as an extension of living an exciting life; the same way a tennis racket, a snowboard, or a hand to hold is an extension of one's passions. He lives in Tampa, Florida, and one day hopes to spend an extended amount of time living abroad.

Barbara Summerhawk writes in longhand from her deck in the Oregon Sisikiyou mountains and her table in her Kiyose house. She is currently teaching aikido in Uruguay....

Shōzō Torii was a member of the VOU Club comprised of poets and artists. The selections included here come from the chapbooks *Desert of the Back* and *Alphabet*

Trap, where each poem takes a human character after a letter of the alphabet, from A to Z. He became an independent publisher of splendid books made by bookmaker Ohie Toshio and editor of the journal exquisitely made of Japanese paper, *TRAP*. He named his press Kaijinsha.

Ilias Tsagas is a Greek poet writing in English and in Greek. His poems have appeared in journals including *Apogee*, *Ambit*, *Under the Radar*, *Poetry Wales*, *FU Review*, *The Shanghai Literary Review*, and *Plumwood Mountain*, and in anthologies including *Addiction and Recovery* by Acid Bath Publishing, *Deviance* by Toothgrinder Press, and *Disease* by Carnaval Press.

Joy Waller is a Canadian writer and editor based in Tokyo. She is the author of *Pause :: Heartbeat* (2019), and her work has appeared in *SAND*, *The Fiddlehead*, *The Malahat Review*, *Best Canadian Stories 2021*, and others. She is also an editor of the Tokyo Poetry Journal and co-host of Drunk Poets See God. www.joywaller.com IG: @joyous. waller

Alex Watson is an Associate Professor at the School of Arts and Letters at Meiji University, Japan. Originally from the UK, after receiving a D.Phil. in English from the University of York in 2007 and working for the University of Edinburgh and several other institutions, he arrived in Japan in 2011. Alex's research interests include British Romanticism, marginalia, paratexts, Gothic fiction, and cinema. His major publications include *British Romanticism in Asia: The Reception, Translation, and Transformation of Romantic Literature in India and East Asia* (2019) co-edited with Laurence Williams, and *Romantic Marginality: Nation and Empire on the Borders of the Page* (2012). He is also co-organizer of Tokyo Humanities Café.

Duncan Whom does performance art and drag cabaret, directs horror movies, and lives in Kamakura with his partner and cat.

Brian Wood-Koiwa has lived/worked and travelled around the world, in places such as Qatar, Ecuador, Thailand, Australia, and as a Peace Corps Volunteer in central Africa (Cameroun, Gabon, and the Republic of Congo), before settling down in Tokyo. He has been living in Tokyo for over 20 years, so his art is inspired by the beautiful ugliness and ugly beauty of The City. Brian calls his creative style "UrbanWeird": emphasizing the phantasmagorical of the seemingly urban mundane mixed with the Japanese aesthetic philosophy of Wabi-Sabi. www.urbanweird. com IG: @urbanweirdphoto

Yowen Xan was born in the Caribbean, raised in Canada, and educated in Japan and China. He traverses your borders and tramples your boundaries, and he is not sorry. He indulges all of life's pleasures and refuses none. Just as Hassan ibn Thabit, he was once leaped upon by a female jinn in the street, compelled to utter three verses of poetry, and thereafter became a poet. He is inter alia... a practitioner of bibliolatry and worships the works of Arundathi Roy and Ngugi wa Thiongo, among others... an enthusiast for modern western hip-hop and classical Sino Japanese poetry... a lover of all things Kansai, whither he has transplanted himself and sunk roots... a scribbler writing about complicated love, the remaking of culture and identity, the pain of migration and detention, and a geriatric Japan that needs people to migrate, make love, and remake themselves and this country. xan.237@gmail.com, IG: @yowenxan

Daisuke Yakumo. Born and raised in Tokyo. Extreme socialite and recluse. Maintains mental balance by writing. A follower of Rimbaud, Salinger, Kerouac, Bukowski, Steinbeck... and fire and stars.